W9-ARC-695

DATE DUE

NF

Wright, Chris

Java

DUE DATE   1C05   15.95

Java

SECOND EDITION

Chris Wright

TEACH YOURSELF BOOKS

For UK orders: please contact Bookpoint Ltd, 78 Milton Park, Abingdon, Oxon OX14 4TD. Telephone: (44) 01235 400414, Fax: (44) 01235 400454. Lines are open 9.00 – 6.00, Monday to Saturday, with a 24-hour message answering service. E-mail address: orders@bookpoint.co.uk

For USA and Canada orders: please contact NTC/Contemporary Publishing, 4255 West Touhy Avenue, Lincolnwood, Illinois 60646-1975, USA. Telephone: (847) 679 5500, Fax: (847) 679 2494.

Long renowned as the authoritative source for self-guided learning – with more than 40 million copies sold worldwide – the *Teach Yourself* series includes over 200 titles in the fields of languages, crafts, hobbies, business and education.

British Library Cataloguing in Publication Data
A catalogue record for this title is available from the British Library.

Library of Congress Catalog Card Number: On file

First published in UK 2000 by Hodder Headline Plc, 338 Euston Road, London, NW1 3BH

First published in US 2000 by NTC/Contemporary Publishing, 4255 West Touhy Avenue, Lincolnwood (Chicago), Illinois 60646-1975 USA.

The 'Teach Yourself' name and logo are registered trade marks of Hodder & Stoughton Ltd. Computer hardware and software brand names mentioned in this book are protected by their registered trademarks and are acknowledged.

Typeset by MacDesign, Southampton
Printed in Great Britain for Hodder & Stoughton Educational, a division of Hodder Headline Plc, 338 Euston Road, London NW1 3BH by Cox & Wyman, Reading, Berkshire.

Impression number	10 9 8 7 6 5 4 3 2
Year	2005 2004 2003 2002 2001 2000

CONTENTS

ACKNOWLEDGEMENTS

Of the many products referred to in this book, those that are registered trademarks are acknowledged as being the property of their owners:

Sun Microsystems, Unix, Linux, SunSoft, Java, JavaScript, Netscape, Microsoft, MSDOS, Windows, Windows 98, Paintshop Pro, Graphics Workshop, TextPad

Thanks are also due to all the artists whose music has provided a soundtrack for the hours, nights and weeks of programming and editing – Brian Eno, Russell Mills, Bill Laswell and John Cale, to name but a few.

Thanks are especially due to Brenda McWalters, whose support throughout the course of this and other projects has been unstinting.

Disclaimer

Feel free to use any of the code you find in this book. This is a book to be treated as you would a recipe book – some of the dishes are complex, others are not. Be aware that if you *do* use code from this book, all of the programs have been written to show how a *part* of the language works. For this reason error checking, which is a vital part of industrial-strength programming, has been kept to a minimum. Bear in mind that you must provide for user mistakes as well as computer problems. For example, the calculator program would in the real world test for the user inputting invalid data; the web browser would test for the user growing impatient and sending a second request before the first has been dealt with. This type of eventuality can cause serious problems, so ignore at your peril!

1 | GETTING STARTED

AIMS OF THIS CHAPTER

This book is aimed at people with little or no programming knowledge, who have experience of surfing the web and have come across Java and who wish to take things a stage further. You will discover what Java is, how it relates to JavaScript, where it comes from, how to obtain it and install it and what hardware and additional software you need to run it. You will also learn the basic skills required to create programs that conform to the Java2 implementation.

1.1 What is Java?

Java and the World Wide Web arrived at a time when object-oriented programming was a black art, the syntax of C++ being enough to deter all but the most determined individuals. One undesirable side-effect of this was that C++ struggled to define a usable set of libraries and programmers and organizations developed their own, often highly idiosyncratic, ways of solving programming problems.

Java and the WWW promise to change this situation for ever. Java carries its own reusable code in extensive package libraries and it is possible now to join programming news groups that specialize in particular aspects of programming, where advice can be sought from a pool of hundreds of programmers. Web sites such as **Developer.com** maintain vast repositories of Java programs, many of which are supplied with the original code. It is now possible to build a research period into the development cycle, where different people's advice and approaches can be compared and evaluated.

Java is a large language, and it is not my intention to cover all of it with this book. Rather, I intend to provide the basic building blocks and a method of working that allows the beginner to create working applets and applications.

In the swiftly moving world of computing, Java is probably the most exciting development since Windows made computers accessible to everyone. It has become inextricably associated with the WWW and in the Servlet API and Java Server Pages provides many of the mechanisms that make web sites truly interactive.

For business, Java offers a means of becoming more competitive. It offers through the Internet the ability to create a marketing presence on a global basis, to offer product support globally at no increase in cost and – in the case of digital products – the ability to deliver the product straight to the customer, charge their credit card and file their details immediately.

Java also offers a solution to the desktop dichotomy; before the Internet, software products had to be provided with a front end for every platform, but this is emphatically no longer the case. With drivers available for most database systems, Java can provide remote access to databases globally, including legacy systems, and the front end will be the same for all customers, regardless of platform.

In telecommunications, Java will further enable the intelligent office. A range of Java chips for cellular phones, printers, fax machines and computers will standardize the connectivity between desktop devices such as PCs and printers and cellular devices such as mobile phones. A set-top box will be provided for the television set, enabling it to be used as a communications centre.

Looking further ahead, with JINI network connectivity, Java can provide the mechanisms for the house of the future, providing intelligence for all the electronic gadgetry that we surround ourselves with. The fridge might generate our shopping list, the TV could be made to automatically adjust its volume when conversation starts, a light may come on when you take a book from the bookcase. These things will be possible sooner rather than later, because the Java Virtual Machine (JVM) can be used anywhere, on any electronic apparatus.

Java is a portable, interpreted, object-oriented programming language. It is *portable* in that the same program will run on any platform running the JVM – unlike C++, for example, which has to be recompiled for every platform. This gives the language a considerable advantage because code need only be written once – saving development time – and because we can send a Java program to any computer without worrying about whether it will work or not. On the Internet, this gives Java a unique advantage.

It is *interpreted* in that, when a Java program is compiled, it is compiled to byte code, rather than machine code. This characteristic gives it portability, but it is achieved at the cost of speed. You can view byte code as a 'halfway house' between the original program and the machine instructions that actually run the computer. It is the responsibility of the JVM to interpret the byte code for the specific platform. In other words the JVM will optimize code for the platform it is installed on.

Java is *object oriented* in that it adheres to the object-oriented development paradigm. The development of programming languages can be seen as a journey away from the machine – assembler language – towards the human way of doing things. Object orientation is an attempt to mimic the way that humans see the world. The theory is that if we can do this successfully, then designing a computer program should become an intuitive as well as an intellectual exercise. Objects can be viewed as components and if we look at the construction industry – one of the oldest human activities – we see that the component idea has been around for a long time. If we are building a house, and need a water supply, we send for a plumber. In programming terms the plumber would be an object, knowing the detail about water in houses. We, as the architect, don't need to know the details, only the plumber's phone number. We will look more closely at object orientation in Chapter 3.

Java is not to be confused with JavaScript. JavaScript is an interpreted scripting language which is object based and uses similar imperative programming techniques. JavaScript is used exclusively as a web-based tool to enhance the interaction of web pages viewed in a browser such as Netscape or Internet Explorer. Although there are similarities between the two, Java is a much more powerful tool for the web developer.

1.2 The future – programming the Enterprise

Trends noticeable in the present include the widespread use of intranets within corporate computing. The use of intranets invites widespread dissemination of information through the use of databases. All information retrievable from a company's computer will be current. There will be no more generations of paper memos to juggle. Java provides methods to seamlessly integrate relational databases into the web browser, so the browser becomes the front end for a database.

JDBC stands for Java Database Connectivity. Current trends imply that much web content will be supplied by large databases storing and manipulating data as it becomes available. This normally requires some sort of 'middleware' to govern the process of a web browser 'talking to' a database. Java 1.1 provided a new package, **java.sql** that allows the programmer to directly interrogate a relational database in the language it understands – SQL. The JDBC provides a set of APIs (application programming interfaces) that make this process a simple one of transferring data between databases and Java objects.

There is also a demand for less programmer-intensive languages. The success of Visual programming and the widespread use of 4GLs has made rapid application development a reality. Java is not a visual programming environment, although such IDEs (integrated development environments) are available. What Java offers is an advanced (and still evolving) set of packages containing ready-made classes for programmers to use. The Java AWT, for example, provides widgets in the form of scroll bars, menus, dialogue boxes, etc., which can be easily integrated into programs and which are guaranteed to run on any platform supporting a JVM. Sun brought Java closer to the 4GL way of working with the introduction in JDK1.1 of JavaBeans.

JavaBeans is a framework for defining reusable modular software components. The specification says that a Java Bean is a reusable software component that can be manipulated visually in a builder tool. The idea here is to take the object-oriented notion of reuse by abstraction and repackage it with reuse by specification. Java Beans can be customized, their properties altered and reused in a specific program. The builder tool is called a Bean Box. Examples provided by Sun include the ubiquitous juggling penguin; however, there are more flexible uses. At the lowest level, reuse is already provided for in the shape of AWT components such as scroll bars and textFields. JavaBeans will enable reuse at a much higher level. We will be able to package high-level GUI components (e.g. a calculator) as Beans and, by reuse, reduce our development costs. JavaBeans is likely to combine the power of 4GL rapid application development tools with the flexibility of an object-oriented programming language in a way that Microsoft have only hinted at with Visual Basic and ActiveX.

1.3 Where can I get Java?

If your operating system is Windows NT/95/98, or Solaris, you can download Java free from Sun at: *http://www.javasoft.com/*

If your operating system is Linux, you will require a port of the JDK designed for that operating system. Information on current ports can be found at *http://www.blackdown.org/* – the Blackdown Organisation's web site.

The version of Java used in this book is found in the Java Developers' Kit (J2SE) or Java2 SDK. It comes with an installation program which guides the user through the process. It may be downloaded from java.sun.com at: *http://java.sun.com/products/jdk/1.2/*

1.4 What equipment do I need?

If you are running Windows, you need at least a 486/DX or faster processor with at least 32 megabytes RAM, although 48 megabytes of RAM are recommended. You will also require 65 megabytes of free disk space before attempting to install the Java2 SDK software. If you also install the separate documentation download bundle (this is advisable), you need an additional 90 megabytes of free disk space.

1.5 How do I learn to program Java?

Java is not a difficult language to learn; it is a difficult language to *master*. The reality is that learning to program is more unforgiving than learning a language, but shares with linguistics the ability to build abstractions out of small structures governed by rigid syntactical rules. The key to learning to program is confidence and for that reason this book focuses on programs that you might encounter in the real world, rather than on programs that are artificially contrived to illustrate a point about programming technique (I have used this type of program only where there is a danger that a vital point may be lost if embedded in a larger program). Chapter 2, for example, where the ground rules are established, contains little in the way of real-world examples.

The traditional method of teaching to program was first to teach the programmer the basic skills and then have him or her work on checking and correcting other people's code for a period, until they were considered trustworthy to write code themselves. The benefit of this experience was that the programmer would see how experienced programmers dealt with the language – in particular, how they used the language to solve abstract problems. For this reason, many of the chapters begin with fairly advanced examples. Do not worry if you don't understand the example straight away: the important thing is that you try to trace the logic of the program as you work through the chapter. All should be clear in the end.

Used in isolation this book will not teach you to be a programmer. It will teach you several things about Java, but you need to supplement the book with practice – do attempt the exercises; they are designed to allow you to build upon the 'story so far', and often draw on techniques demonstrated in earlier chapters.

To get the best out of the language, the reader should join at least one news group, and bookmark several of the reference sites indicated in the appendix. Java can be a complex language and you will save much time by bookmarking in your web browser the Java API documentation distributed with the SDK, which lists all of the packages supplied with Java – and, more importantly, lists the methods available to each class, indicating argument types and return types.

SUMMARY

✓ Java is a programming language, not an application. Like all languages it possesses its own rules governing syntax and grammar, but unlike many programming languages it provides extensive libraries of predefined classes allowing the programmer the best of the 'plug in and play' approach typified by 4GLs, combined with the flexibility and power of languages such as C++.

✓ Java is distributed free by Sun Microsystems. It was designed originally as a language to use to enable electronic components to communicate. The Internet provided the perfect opportunity for Java as a language and Sun as a company to put up a viable alternative to Microsoft's dominance of the PC world.

✓ There is more information published about Java than any other aspect of computing, except the WWW itself. This is a measure of how enthusiastically people in the computing industry have responded to the existence of a truly multi-platform programming language.

✓ In order to learn to program, you have to program – this cannot be over-emphasized. It is only by use that you will become fluent in Java. Many of the exercises in the book are designed for you to develop and customize for your own use.

Exercises

❶ Download Java from the Sun web site at:
   http://java.sun.com/products/jdk/1.2/

❷ Print out the ReadMe files included with the distribution – and read them!

❸ Install Java on your computer.

❹ Join the news groups **comp.lang.java.programmer** and **comp.lang.java.gui**

❺ Bookmark the Developer.com web site at:
   http://www.developer.com/

❻ Bookmark the Java API Guide in the docs subdirectory of your installation.

2 | PROGRAMMING BASICS

AIMS OF THIS CHAPTER

The primary aim of this chapter is to create and compile simple Java programs.

In order to succeed in this we need to look at the language syntax and understand the meaning and functions of allowed data types, reserved words, the use of variables, operators and the concept and practice of program control. We will introduce each new concept by looking at the way in which it works inside an actual program. You can compile the programs and then you will see the effect of altering certain statements within the program. The examples will illustrate the use of various language elements and you can use the examples as a basis for building larger programs.

At the end of the chapter there is a list of exercises. Try to complete these – you might have to do some research in order to find solutions to some of the problems. Don't worry if you have trouble with some questions; you can always come back to them later.

2.1 A first Java program

This section assumes that you will be working with Windows. The commands that are represented in italics are the same for all versions of the JDK, whether your platform is Unix, Windows 95 or Apple. There are a number of excellent programmer's editors on the market – try downloading TextPad from www.textpad.com – which has macros that allow you to compile and run Java programs from the editor and features line numbers, keyword highlighting and automatic indentation amongst other features.

For those without an Internet connection, you can work with Java perfectly easily by using multiple windows – one to edit in, one to compile and one to run the program. This practice will save you time, because you can use the right-hand arrow key on the keyboard to repeat the previous command.

Open a DOS window and type:

```
edit MyFirst.java
```

Now enter the code below, exactly as it is written here.

```
import java.io.*;
class MyFirst
{
    public static void main(String[ ] args)
    {
        /* print something to the output stream */
        System.out.println ("Hello Birds, Hello Sky!!");
    }
}
```

Save the file and then compile the program in a second DOS window. Change directories until you are in the same directory as your program file, then enter at the command prompt the line:

```
javac MyFirst.java
```

If you have entered the file correctly, you should receive no error message. If you have made a mistake, you will get a message in the format:

```
MyFile.java:7: missing {
```

This would tell you that you have missed out the bracket on line 7. If this is the case, alter your source file, save it and recompile the program.

If your compilation is successful, run the program (from a third window) by entering the line:

```
java MyFirst
```

You should see a line of text printed to the screen, saying:

    Hello Birds, Hello Sky!!

The line:

    System.out.println ("Hello Birds, Hello Sky!!");

is the one which determines the actual output. If you alter the text between the inverted commas, you will get a different message when you recompile and run the program.

The words before the brackets represent a call to a method – **println( )** – in the object **System.out**. The method takes a string as an argument, which is contained within the brackets. The inverted commas tell the compiler where the beginning and end of the string are. The class **System** is imported from the **java.io** package, a library of predefined classes implementing input and output. **out** is a variable of type **OutputStream**, and the method **println( )** automatically moves to a new line. There is also a method **print( )**, which will continue to output to the same line. **print( )** is usually followed by a second method, **System.flush( )**, which 'forces' the output to the screen.

The words *object*, *method*, *argument* and *string*, are probably new to you. There are two concepts fundamental to object-oriented programming in Java: *objects* and *variables*. Objects contain methods and data which allow them to communicate with other objects and the system. Variables are defined as being of a certain data type – such as *char* (character) or *int* (integer) – and contain values of that type. A variable may be found inside an object, or may be passed to an object in the form of an *argument*. As Java is an object-oriented language, everything is defined as *classes*; when a class is compiled and run it forms an *object*, which exists in memory until the program ends or until the program has no further use for it. In this simple example, we have only one class, which is defined within the lines:

    class MyFirst
    {
        // class definition - variables and methods go here
    }

This particular class has only one method, called **main.** Every Java application (but not applets) must have a method called main, which can take arguments if required. The line:

```
public static void main(String[ ] args)
```

would store such arguments as are given it in an array of **Strings** called **args**. We will be covering this process in more detail later in the book, so for the moment we will take this line as written.

The definition of the method is given between the curly brackets. Note the indenting of the curly brackets relative to the margin. This is not required by the compiler, but leaving one bracket out is probably the most common error in programming, and if you can see the pairs by scanning the page it is easy to spot the missing one.

Finally any text contained between the /* and */ symbols is a comment. Comments are not processed by the compiler and are intended to preserve sanity, both yours and anyone who comes along afterwards and reads the code. You will find that if you come back to a long program after a month or two, you will have forgotten the thought processes that went into it. Comments are an excellent way of preserving these thoughts for future use. A single line comment is indicated by the symbol //.

```
// This is a single line comment
```

To summarize: if we want to write a program to print output to the screen, we need to go through the following steps.

❶ Identify the class and the packages you need to import from:

```
import java.io.*;
class MyFirst
{
}
```

❷ Identify the class methods and insert them between the classes' containing brackets:

```
class MyFirst
{
    public static void main(String[ ] args)
    {
    }
}
```

❸ Implement the methods:

```
class MyFirst
{
   public static void main(String[ ] args)
   {
      System.out.println ("Hello Birds, Hello Sky!!");
   }
}
```

❹ Comment as required:

```
/* This is my first program, it is designed to
demonstrate a simple program structure
Author: Chris Wright 11.02.XX
*/

import java.io.*;

class MyFirst
{
   public static void main(String[ ] args)
   {
      System.out.println ("Hello Birds, Hello Sky!!");
   }
}
```

❺ Compile (**javac ClassName.java**).

❻ Correct if compilation is unsuccessful.

❼ Run (**java ClassName**).

❽ Correct if unsatisfactory.

For a program of this size, it is appropriate to put the comments in last. When you start creating larger programs, you should comment as you go – with programming, you can never make life too easy!

2.2 Data types

Java is a very strongly typed language. This means that when we want to store a value in memory we have to state a specific type. This helps the computer to allocate an appropriate amount of storage.

There are eight *primitive data types*: six *numeric*, one *alphabetic* and one known as *Boolean*.

The numeric types consist of:

- ◆   **int** which is the most commonly used, requiring 4 bytes of storage and covering whole numbers between –2,147,483,648 to 2,147,483,647.

- ◆   **short** which uses half the storage (2 bytes) and covers numbers between -32,768 and 32,767.

- ◆   **byte** which uses half as much storage as short (1 byte) and covers –128 to +127

- ◆   **long** which uses 8 bytes of storage and covers numbers between –9,223,372,036,854,775,808L and +9,223,372,036,854,775,807L.

These integer types cover whole numbers only and are important for two reasons. First, they give us the opportunity to save memory requirements in large programs, thus giving us faster performance, and second, in Java, these ranges give us platform independence because they are known to work on all existing machines.

To store fractions we need two extra types:

- ◆   **float** which requires 4 bytes of storage and covers fractions with 7 significant digits.

- ◆   **double** which requires 8 bytes of storage and covers fractions with 15 significant digits.

Again the reason for having two types of fractions is for economy of storage.

The character type in Java is called **char** and is used to contain single characters, which are specified between single quotation marks ('Y' or 'N'). To contain longer sequences of characters we use an object called **String** which contains characters specified between double quotation marks ("Yes" or "No").

The last primitive data type is **Boolean** which contains the values *false* and *true*. This type is used for testing when there are only two possible outcomes.

2.3 Variables

To use the data types in a program, we need to explicitly declare a variable of a particular type. If, for example, we want to write a program to calculate my salary, we could declare a variable to contain the calculated value of my salary, and would do this by writing:

```
private double mySalary;
```

Storage is usually declared at the top of a program, before the first method. Any data declared here will be accessible to all methods used by the class. Because it is preceded by the keyword **private**, it will not be accessible to other classes. Some methods require their own storage for variables that are of interest only to that method. These may be declared in the same way, inside the method itself.

We can use any word for a variable, except for what are known as *reserved words*. These are words that are meaningful to the Java compiler. There are 59 reserved words, including all of the data types – for a full list see Appendix 1.

It is good practice in programming to choose composite words that mean something for variables, unless they are numbers used for controlling loops, which are typically placed in variables i, j or k. The choice of variable name should help to make the program more readable.

If we needed more variables of the same type, we could write:

```
double mySalary, myBaseSalary, myOverTime;
```

This would allow us to discover the value of our full salary by adding the value of the overtime to the base salary.

To compute the value of the overtime we would need two more variables:

```
double hourlyRate;
int hours;
```

We now need to give the variable a value. We do this by a process known as *assignment*. To continue with the salary example, we would write:

```
myBaseSalary = 10000;
// Note – first letter lower case –        no commas
hourlyRate = 5.50;
hours = 10;
```

Looking at these declarations, it is easy to see that we can compute the value of the remaining variables by manipulating the ones we have assigned.

2.4 Operators

In Java the allowed operators are:

+   Addition

−   Subtraction

*   Multiplication

/   Division

%   Integer Remainder

To return once again to the Salary declarations, we can now manipulate the variables:

```
myOverTime = hourlyRate * hours;
mySalary = myBaseSalary + myOverTime;
```

In addition to these, we have *increment operators* (++) and *decrement operators* (−−). These are used to add 1 to or subtract 1 from the value of a variable. The use of these operators will be covered in the section on control later in this chapter.

You may be wondering how we can multiply a variable of type **float** by one of type **int**?

The answer is that Java assumes the answer to be in the larger type – in this case **float**.

This is true for the whole hierarchy of numeric types. For example:

```
double * (float, long, int, short, byte) = double
    float * (long, int, short, byte) = float
    long * (int, short, byte) = long
    int * (short, byte) = int
    short * byte = short
```

This is fine, but what happens when we want the answer to be in the smaller type? The answer is found in a process called *casting*. When casting down the hierarchy this has to be done explicitly:

```
double mySalary = 10000.65;
int approxSalary = (int) mySalary;
```

The value held in the variable approxSalary is 10000. Note that the value is truncated, not rounded.

Relational and *Boolean operators* are used to compare values. The allowed operators are:

==   is equal to

!=   is not equal to

<   is less than

>   is more than

<=   is less than or equal to

>=   is greater than or equal to

&& AND

|| OR

Armed with these operators, we can organize some conditional behaviour:

```
IF mySalary is less than myExpenses and myOverTime is
    equal to 0
THEN print "Bankruptcy Looms!"
```

This statement is in the form of pseudocode, a simple logical structure which is sometimes used to clarify matters before coding a complex problem. However, before converting this into Java, we need to examine control structures.

2.5 Control structures

This section describes the use of control structures in Java, much of which is logically identical to C and C++. Each subsection will show the control structure in the context of a program and explain any new features as they occur.

2.5.1 if...else

```java
import java.io.*;
class PayCheck
// note – programmer defined class names begin with capitals
{
    public static void main(String[ ] args)
    {
        double mySalary, myBaseSalary, myOverTime, hourlyRate;
        int hours;

        myBaseSalary = 10000;
        hourlyRate = 5.50;
        hours = 10;

// we'll use a control structure to check for overtime payments
        if (hours > 0 )
        {
            myOverTime = hourlyRate * hours;
            mySalary = myBaseSalary + myOverTime;
        } // end if
        else
        {
            mySalary = myBaseSalary;
        } // end else
        // Now print out the result
        System.out.println ("Your salary this week is £" + mySalary);
    } // end method definition
} /* Leave a space behind end class bracket so we can
        easily tell it apart */
```

This program illustrates the use of the **if** statement. Notice that the condition upon which the first statement block is predicated is in brackets. The statement block can contain any number of statements. If the condition is not met, the program drops straight through to the **else** statement block.

Compile and run this program as it is written, then change the value of hours from 10 to 0 and compile and run it a second time. Try this for any other value of hours and watch the output change.

Note that it is not essential to have an **else** block: the simplest use of this structure is:

```
if (condition)
   { result if condition is true }
```

2.5.2 while

```
import java.io.*;
class MyFinance
{
   public static void main(String[ ] args)
   {
      // declare storage for variables
      double mySalary, myExpenses, myOverdraft, mySaving,
      surplus;
      int years;
      // initialise variables
      mySalary = 10000;
      myExpenses = 9500;
      myOverdraft = 20000;
      mySaving = 0;
      years = 0;

      //calculate a value for surplus
      surplus = mySalary – myExpenses;

      // test for the condition then execute block
      while (mySaving < myOverdraft)
      {
         mySaving = mySaving + surplus;
         years++;
      }
      // print out the result
      System.out.println ("It is going to take you " + years +
      "years to pay off your overdraft!");
   }
}
```

There are a few new things to note in this program.

First, the setting of variables to 0 at the top of the program. In the previous program, every variable was allocated a value, either by initialization at the top of the program or by calculation within the program. In this program, if we look at the value of **mySaving** we can see that it is used before it is given a value by the program. In these circumstances, we must always allocate the variable a value, otherwise the value will be whatever the computer finds in memory allocated to that variable, which could be left over from a previous program!

Second, because we are only using a single method, main, in these classes, the variables may safely be declared inside the main method and will not require the private keyword to restrict their access.

Third, if we examine the **while** statement, we can see that the program tests the condition before it processes the block. If the condition is not true, then the block will be ignored. Test this by allocating **mySaving** a value greater than the overdraft.

Finally, the line

```
mySaving = mySaving + surplus;
```

may look a little strange if you are new to programming. What is happening here is that **mySaving** holds a value. If we want to change the value, it has to be re-assigned. The simplest way to achieve this is to add our surplus for the year on to the original value. This line can also be written as **mySaving += surplus;**, which is arguably even harder to comprehend.

2.5.3 do...while

If we need the program to execute a block of code at least once, we can use another construct, **do...while**:

```
do
  {
      mySaving = mySaving + surplus;
      year ++;
  }
while (mySaving < myOverdraft);
```

This sequence assumes that we do have an overdraft – the **while** condition checks at the end of the loop to see if the loop needs to be processed a second time.

2.5.4 for

Determinate loops are used to support general iteration – for example, counters. This construct is used frequently in Java – it is amazing how many occasions require a counter!

```java
import java.io.*;

class FlatBroke
{
    public static void main(String[ ] args)
    {
        for (int i =10; i= 0; i--)
        {
            System.out.println("Pounds left: £" + i);
        } // end actions depending on counter
        System.out.println("Flat Broke!");
    } // end method
} // end class definition
```

2.5.5 switch

Java also supports a **switch** statement. This gives us a less cumbersome method of dealing with a range of possibilities than using a chain of **if** statements. The important thing to remember about the switch is that the data types it takes are restricted to byte, char, short, int and long. When using double, as in the example, we must cast the double to an int variable.

To return to the salary example:

```java
import java.io.*;
class MyFinance
{
    public static void main(String[ ] args)
    {
        double mySalary, myExpenses, myOverdraft, mySaving,
        surplus;
        int years;

        mySalary = 10000;
        myExpenses = 9500;
```

```
    myOverdraft = 20000;
    mySaving = 0;
    years = 0;

    //calculate a value for surplus
    surplus = mySalary - myExpenses;

    // cast mySalary to int for switch statement
    int payCheck = (int)mySalary;

    //check salary and issue cautionary warning!
    switch (payCheck)
    {
        case 10000:
        System.out.println ("One day you will earn more money!");
        break;

        case 15000:
        System.out.println ("15000 is not a bad salary...");
        break;

        case 20000:
        System.out.println ("You shouldn't really have an
            overdraft!");
        break;

        default:
        // no default behaviour needed, we only need 3
    // messages
        break;
    } // end switch statement
  }
}
```

The **switch** statement here is used to output a message to the screen at particular points on a salary scale. If you change the variable **mySalary** to 10001 no message will be output: the program will drop straight through to the default behaviour (in this case none) and exit the switch statement.

An important feature of this structure is the use of **break** to exit. This can also be applied to the other control structures, to take into account special circumstances that would require a loop to terminate before it had met the condition.

2.5.6 Labelled break

The **break** statement may be used as a way of giving two exit conditions for a loop. For example, in the program above, we may choose to break the loop if the number of years is greater than 100, as it is unlikely that we could pay off an overdraft over 100 years!

```
// contained within method after switch statement
paymentPlan:
    while (mySaving < myOverdraft)
    {
        mySaving = mySaving + surplus;
        years++;
        while (years > 100)
        {
            System.out.println ("You will not be solvent in this
                lifetime!");
            break paymentPlan;
        } // end while

    } // end while
    System.out.println ("It is going to take you more than
        100 years to pay off your overdraft!");
```

This example is called a *labelled break*. The label is **paymentPlan:**, the effect of years exceeding 100 will be to print out the lines "You will not be solvent..." and "It is going to take you more than 100 years to pay off your overdraft". If we omitted the label, only the second **while** statement would terminate; the program would continue calculating the exact number of years it will take to reach solvency. The label must be placed *before* the loop we want to break out of.

2.6 Methods

So far, our classes have had only one method, **main**, and while we are creating only simple programs this is an acceptable approach but as soon as we introduce some complexity into the program it becomes difficult to visualize exactly what a program is doing. Breaking the responsibilities of a class into methods is beneficial because the program becomes easier to understand and easier to visualize. In the example below we can follow the logic in the method **main**.

```java
import java.io.*;

class Methods
{
    public static int square(int x)
    // Takes an integer x as an argument
    {
        return x*x;          // returns the result as an integer
    }

    public static void display(int a)
    // Takes an integer and displays it
    {
        System.out.println("The answer is: " + a);
    }

    public static void main(String[ ] args)
    {
        int number=4;        // initialises the number to 4
        int answer=square(number);
        // calls the method square to deliver a value
        display(answer); // Displays the value found in answer
    }
}
```

The declaration of the method

```java
public static int square(int x)
```

means that the method is **public** (i.e., it can be used by any object derived from this class), it is **static** to ensure that any of the classes other members can access it, returns a value of type **int** and is passed a value of type **int**.

A method can be passed a variable to do some computing with, and can return a result. In this simple example, the line:

```java
int answer=square(number);
```

is the same as if we had written

```
int answer=number * number;
```

By defining the calculation as a method, we gain the flexibility of being able to pass any number into it, at any point in our program, without worrying about how the calculation is done.

Part of the beauty of this approach is that it saves us from endless repetition. We will consider methods in greater depth in Chapter 3.

2.7 Arrays

An *array* is an example of a data structure. We can think of a simple one-dimensional array as a numbered list of variables of the same type. When we declare an array, we declare it as being of a data type, and then give it a variable name and a length:

```
String[ ] dinnerGuests = new String[8];
```

```
dinnerGuests[0] = "Fred";
dinnerGuests[1] = "Jane";
// repeat up to ...
dinnerGuests[7] = "Ruth";
```

You will notice that the first guest, Fred, is at position [0] in the array. Arrays in Java run from 0 to (size −1). In other words, an array of 10 integers would consist of positions 0–9.

This initialization of the array is a little long-winded for a large party, a shorter way would be to write:

```
String dinnerGuests[ ] = {"Fred", "Jane", "Michael",
    "Brenda", "Chris", "Geraldine", "Gary", "Ruth"};
```

To access an element of an array, we refer to it by its index:

```
System.out.println(dinnerGuests[3]);
```

would print "Brenda" to the screen.

By using a loop, we can print out all the names:

```
for (int i=0; i<=7; i++)
    {
    System.out.println("Guest number " + ( i + 1 ) + " is " +
        dinnerGuests[i]);
    }
```

2.8 Strings

We have made several references to string as if it were a data type. This is not the case – strings in Java are represented as a class, not as an array of characters. Because they are a class, they have methods such as **length( )** and **substring( )** which allow us to manipulate and compare them.

```java
String virtue = "Good";
String sin = "Greed";

if (virtue == sin)
{
    System.out.println("My name is Gordon Gecko!!");
}
else
{
    System.out.println(virtue);
}
```

The code above compares the two strings and hopefully finds that Greed is not equal to Good. It then prints the word "Good" to the screen.

The method length allows us to deposit the length of a string into an integer variable:

```java
int x = virtue.length( );
```

We can create new strings by taking the substring of an existing string. For example:

```java
String glue = virtue.substring(0, 3);
```

gives the new string glue a value of "Goo".

We can also alter an existing string by assigning it to itself:

```java
String virtue=virtue.substring(0,3);
```

What was "good" is now "goo".

SUMMARY

✓ We now have the building blocks needed to build quite sophisticated programs. We have covered reserved words (see Appendix 1), looked at the kind of words which we might choose to use as variable names, allowed data types, the use and assignment of variables, operands and operators, noted the advantages of using methods and the concept and practice of program control. In addition we have taken a brief look at arrays and strings. .

✓ All of the control structures we have used can be nested. This means that we can insert a **while** loop, for example, inside another control structure. This can be quite difficult to keep track of, so take care! At least one of the following exercises will require nested loops of some kind in order to reach an elegant solution.

✓ We have also looked at good programming practice as we have moved through the chapter. Comments can be more useful than you might think at this stage. Other good programming habits are the use of logical variable names, appropriate capitalization, using white space to separate your blocks of code and indenting blocks so that you can easily see where one block ends and a new one begins. By paying attention to the way you lay out a program you will save yourself hours of frustration – there is no sadder sight than a programmer unable to read their own program!

Exercises

❶ Write a program to print a line of five asterisks across the page.

❷ Using a control structure, change the program to print a square made up of asterisks.

❸ Modify this program to create a right-angled triangle.

❹ Write a program to create an equilateral triangle. (Hint: you can print blank spaces.)

❺ Write a program to store three names in an array. If two of the names are identical the program should emit the warning "This password has already been chosen!"

3 | CLASSES AND OBJECTS

AIMS OF THIS CHAPTER

Now that we have a firm grasp of control structures in simple programs, we need to start building some larger structures so that we can see them in use. Everything we have done so far has included a line:

class ClassName

This line tells the compiler to create a class file called *ClassName*.class (or whatever name we decided to give the program). This chapter will explain the relationship between classes and objects, introduce the ideas of encapsulation, composition and inheritance and explain why these concepts are useful, explain the use of interfaces and how we can use all this to build bigger and better programs. It will show how to design the most appropriate classes, how to create classes and how to use them.

This chapter will also look at the various packages of classes supplied with the JDK. One of the great strengths of Java is the abundance of reusable code that is supplied in the class libraries. Every time we use the line:

import java.io.*

we have made available to our program any of the methods we choose to use from the java.io class package. We will look at the class packages available with Java and discover that reinventing the wheel is neither desirable nor necessary with object-oriented programming.

3.1 An object-oriented program

What is an object? The classes that we have constructed so far are *definitions* of objects – the object does not exist until it is instantiated by running the code. So far we have used programs with only one class, so only one object has been created. However, the power of objects lies in the fact that they contain or encapsulate their own data and methods. The implication of this is that if we define one class and instantiate it several times, we get several different objects, each with its own set of data and methods. If we designed a class to describe a bank account, we could use it many times to set up individual bank accounts. If we design code to describe an aeroplane, we can create an airforce. The following code is intended only as a demonstration of the power of object-oriented programming; it is incomplete for simplicity's sake and exaggerated for clarity's sake!

```
import java.awt.*;
import java.awt.image.*;

abstract class Aeroplane extends Object
// create an aeroplane template - an abstract class would //
never be instantiated, only used to derive specialized
// classes from.
{
    // give it some necessary data
    private int engines;
    private int seats;
    private int fuel;

    // tell it where it is on the screen
    int x, y;

    //construct an object
    public Aeroplane(int engines, int seats, int fuel)
    {
        this.engines = engines;
        this.seats = seats;
        this.fuel = fuel;
    }
    public abstract void Draw(Graphics g, ImageObserver o);
```

```
} // end class definition

class Airliner extends Aeroplane
{
    private int maxPassengers;

    public Airliner(int engines, int seats, int fuel, int
       maxPassengers)
    {
       super(engines, seats, fuel);
       this.maxPassengers = maxPassengers;
    }

    public void Draw(Graphics g, ImageObserver o)
    {
       // Graphics code goes here
    }

} // ends class definition

class Fighter extends Aeroplane
{
    private int guns;

    public Fighter(int engines, int seats, int fuel, int guns)
    {
       super(engines, seats, fuel);
       this.guns = guns;
    }

    public void Draw(Graphics g, ImageObserver o)
    {
       // Graphics code goes here
    }

} // ends class definition
```

This example demonstrates a way we might choose to implement a number of different aeroplanes. We have chosen aeroplanes because all aeroplanes have some things in common, which gives us an opportunity to abstract those qualities that all aeroplanes share and to use them as a template for building any type of aeroplane, thus saving us the tedium of coding masses of identical code for each type of aeroplane. The first class **aeroplane** is the one which contains the data and methods we can share amongst all aeroplanes. Since it is only a template, we designate it **abstract**. We will never instantiate an object of type **aeroplane**, only copy it into other objects. This technique is demonstrated in our second and third classes; the effect of the line

```
class Airliner extends Aeroplane
```

is to give our class **Airliner** access to all the data and methods of our abstract class **Aeroplane**. This means that all we have to do is to give our new class the data that makes it different (i.e. the number of seats) and we have a fully functional airliner. Similarly the third class, **Fighter**, is given guns. It is important to note that **Fighter** would not get the extra seats, unless it extended **Airliner** instead of **Aeroplane**. The inheritance hierarchy in this case looks like Figure 3.1.

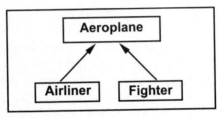

Figure 3.1 Inheritance from superclass Aeroplane

This is a very simplistic example of inheritance, and assumes a great deal – for instance where did the gun come from? How does the engine work? The answers to these questions require a section to themselves.

3.2 Introduction to object orientation

In order to understand object orientation fully it is necessary to take a step backwards and examine the history of software engineering and the way in which it is maturing as an industry.

Software engineering is a very youthful industry, and we can look to other industries for possible reflections and clues as to what may happen in the future. If we look at the oldest industry of all, that of construction, we see an interesting phenomenon. That phenomenon is specialization and it is this that enables us to erect structures such as St Paul's Cathedral from scratch, and then to refine the techniques to build bigger and better versions.

If we look more closely at specialization, we can see some ideas that we can use in software engineering. The whole point of specialists is that they are the experts – all anyone else needs to know is where to find them and what they might expect them to do. Object orientation attempts to model this relationship. If we can use an existing class as a basis for another class, then we need to know only where to find it and what we can expect it to do. This is referred to as *inheritance* in software engineering. Inheritance is only one of three ways in which classes can be related.

We have looked at an example that models inheritance. This could be referred to as an *IS A* relationship – an airliner IS A aeroplane. There is another type of relationship that is not so simply modelled – *HAS A*. It would be unlikely that the good people at Sun have modelled classes to provide us with guns and engines for aeroplanes, and yet these are complex pieces, essential to an aeroplane's 'aeroplaneness'. This relationship is termed *composition*. An aeroplane is composed of things of which it categorically is not an example. So, an airliner IS A aeroplane and it HAS A engine. When designing class structures, it is important to get this relationship right in order to optimize the benefits of object orientation. In Figure 3.2 we see that Object B (Car.java) uses Object A (Engine.java) as a component. Object C (Turbo.java) inherits all the attributes of Object A (Engine.java) and adds some more, such as fuel injection.

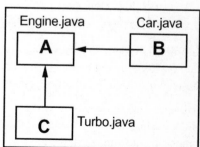

Figure 3.2
Object relationships –
inheritance and composition

Having seen a skeleton of an inheritance model, we can look at the full code for a trivial example of object modelling using composition. Look out for the keyword **new** which indicates that we are creating an instance of the class **Address**.

This is a working example, albeit a trivial one. The files can be compiled separately or together, but keep them in the same directory.

```java
public class Address
{
    private String street;
    private String city;
    private String county;
    private String country;

    // established data storage, now construct class
    // passing it some values as parameters

    public Address(String s, String c, String co, String cou)
    {
        street = s;
        city = c;
        county = co;
        country = cou;
    }

    //provide an accessor method to pass data with
    public String retrieve( )
    {
        return street + "," + city + "," + county + "," + country;
    }

} // end class definition
// This is the main class, which declares an instance of address

import java.io.*;
public class Contact
{
    public static void main(String[ ] args)
    {
        String name = "Joe Soap";
```

```
        // create new object
        Address a = new Address("10 Downing Street",
            "Westminster", "London","England");
        System.out.println("Name=" + name + "Address="+
            a.retrieve( ));
    }
}
```

It should be possible to see, from this trivial example, that a bigger application might be a contact book, which could include classes for name, address and telephone numbers. The general rule when designing classes is that if you have a large number of variables to deal with and some of them are of the same category, such as the lines of an address, then you have a candidate for a further class. The advantages of this approach, which may not be immediately apparent in such a trivial example, are that the details of the address class are hidden from the class that uses it. This means that, if we decide to alter the way in which the display is put onto the screen, we know that all of the code that we need to alter will be found in one place – the **retrieve( )** method of the **Address** class. The internal details of the **retrieve( )** method matter not a jot to the **Contact** class, so we need alter nothing else in the whole program. If for a moment we revert to our previous example of aeroplanes and engines, the benefit should be obvious: we have a single implementation of an engine which might be used by many different aeroplanes. By upgrading that one class, we immediately upgrade any object that is instantiated using that engine – i.e. the whole airforce!

The relationships between classes we have looked at so far include composition and inheritance. There are also circumstances where we would like different classes to behave in partially similar ways. In Java this is dealt with by the use of *interfaces*.

3.2.1 Class relationships

- *Use* – when a class uses the public methods of another class.

- *Inheritance* – when a class is derived from another class.

- *Composition* – when a class is composed of other classes.

When we design an object-oriented program, the first task is to identify the objects (classes), the second to identify the objects' responsibilities (methods). A popular method to establish the beginnings of a class structure is to study the problem description and isolate the nouns. These will often become classes. The verbs will often become methods. Looking at an analysis of an address book, we could say that my *address book* contains the *addresses* of my *contacts*. I want to *add*, *alter* and occasionally *delete contacts*. When I look up the name of *contact* x, I would like the *book* to retrieve their *street*, their *town* and their *telephone number*.

From this simple description we can isolate three objects: **Contact**, **Book** and **Address**. We can assume that **add**, **alter**, **delete** and **lookup** will be the responsibility (methods) of **Book**, the street, town and telephone number are data fields belonging to **Address**, and that the **retrieve** method for these fields will be the responsibility of **Address**.

3.3 Inside objects

Now that we have looked at the big picture, we should look in detail at the code we have used in our examples.

This class is very simple; it merely provides storage for the details of an address, which are passed to it when the class is constructed. It has only one method, which enables it to extract the details of the address from memory and return them as a String to the caller. Notice that the data declarations are given *visibility modifiers*. If a class is to be used with other classes, it is important that the visibility of methods and data is stated. The reason for this is that it helps maintain a consistent interface for other programmers to use.

```
public class Address
{
    private String street;
    private String city;
    private String county;
    private String country;

    // establishes data storage
}
```

The keyword **private** defines the visibility of the data, as seen by other classes. There are three levels of visibility in common use: private, protected and public. *Private* means that no other class can directly manipulate the private data or method. *Protected* means that only classes belonging to the same package or derived from the class containing the protected data or methods can operate on them directly. *Public* means that any other class can manipulate the designated methods or data.

In practice it is customary to keep all data private to a class. This helps the programmer maintain a consistent interface with other classes. In order to access this data, we provide a method called a *getter* or *accessor* method, which returns the data in an appropriate format. This method is public (i.e. other classes can use it). The important thing here is that the interface to this class is provided by the method – once the class is designed, all we need to know is that the address, for example, will be returned as a String. This gives us the freedom to modify the class in the future, without having to alter any other code in programs that use it.

It is important to remember that we have to explicitly declare the number and type of the arguments that are required by this class. We also have to explicitly allocate any argument passed to the class in its constructor method to memory, if we want to be able to access it from other methods. For convenience, we refer to the variables that are passed with different names. This reminds us that the arguments we have declared are method variables (**s**, **c**, **co** and **cou**), and in order to use them elsewhere in the class, we must copy them to instance variables (**street**, **city**, **county** and **country**). We can also call the variables by the same name as in the Aeroplane example and use the **this** operator to place the received value into an internal variable.

```
public class Address
{
    private String street;
    private String city;
    private String county;
    private String country;
```

```
   // instance variables declared, we can provide a constructor
   public Address(String s, String c, String co, String cou)
   {
      // assign arguments to instance variables
      street = s;
      city = c;
      county = co;
      country = cou;
   }
   //class will be instantiated with suitable data when called
```

This part of the class is called a *constructor* method. We provide this method with a number of parameters, which in this case are the details of an address. These details are allocated storage in memory.

```
   //provide an accessor method to pass data with
   public String getAddress( )
   {
      return street + "," + city + "," + county + "," + country;
   }

   } // end class definition
```

The last part of the class is an *accessor* method, which simply enables us to gain access to the data. Another type of method might be termed a '*mutator*' method, which would afford us a way of altering the data.

The next class is a class that is composed with the address class (in other words it HAS A address). Instead of a constructor method, we provide it with a **main** method which does all the processing needed.

```
   public class Contact
   {
      public static void main(String[ ]args)
      {
         String name = "Joe Soap";
         // create new object
         Address a = new address("10 Downing Street",
               "Westminster","London","England");
            System.out.println("Name=" + name + "Address="+
                  a.getAddress( ));
      }
   }
```

The code contained in the main method of class **Contact**, declares a String variable called **name** and creates an object of type **address**, passing to it the details it requires in its constructor method. By creating the class here with the keyword **new**, we automatically call the constructor method of that class. The next line is a call to **System**, to print out the contents of the variable **name**, and to use the **getAddress()** method of our object **a**, in order to print the details of the address. Remember that, until we create an instance of the class, the object does not exist, so we cannot call this method without first declaring a new variable of type address.

3.4 Using class libraries

As we have already mentioned, one of the greatest strengths of Java lies in the extensive libraries. These libraries are subdivided into thematically linked packages, for example **java.io** and **java.net**. A full reference to the contents of these packages can be found in the docs directory of your Java SDK. Nearly all Java programs make use of the packages listed in the Java API, so a complete reference to these packages is an invaluable guide.

The key packages available to the programmer in the basic JDK are these:

♦   **java.beans** – New in JDK1.1, this contains the tools to allow programmers to make their own beans.

♦   **java.io** – Contains classes to enable file creation by applications, and reading and writing to the screen.

♦   **java.lang** – Contains integral objects such as String, class wrappers such as Boolean, Double, Integer and Throwable, which is used in exception handling.

♦   **java.lang.ref** – Introduced in Java2, this defines 'weak references'.

♦   **java.lang.reflect** – New in JDK1.1, this allows classes to inspect themselves via the Member Interface. Beyond the scope of this book.

* **java.math** – New in JDK1.1, and contains extra maths classes allowing arbitrary precision integer and floating point arithmetic.

* **java.net** – Contains a powerful set of networking classes allowing access to URLs, and computer-to-computer communication.

* **java.security** – New in Java2. Defines classes and interfaces for access control and authentication.

* **java.text** – New in JDK1.1. Contains tools to implement internationalization of code.

* **java.util** – Contains utility classes such as vector and stack, date and hashtable, which provide data structures useful to programmers.

In addition to these packages, the Java Foundation Classes provide packages concerned with GUI programming and Graphics, including:

* **java.applet** – Contains the Applet class, which is the superclass of all applets.

* **java.awt** – The Abstract Windowing Toolkit, contains classes in the categories of Graphics (for use with colours, fonts, images, etc.), Components (GUI components such as menus, buttons lists, etc.) and Layout Managers, which control the layout of components within their container objects.

* **javax.swing** – The extended package of GUI components and managers.

To demonstrate the use of class libraries to its most dramatic effect, we need a project which requires a Windows-style interface and which we can continue to develop further on in the book. The project is to build an interface to a game, which we will call Drag Racing. The game will consist of an animation, which will take place in a frame. The user will be able to make bets on the outcome of each race. The components we would need for such an interface would be a button to start the race, an area to enter our bet, an area to view the accumulating losses and an area to post the name of the winning vehicle. It should look something like Figure 3.3.

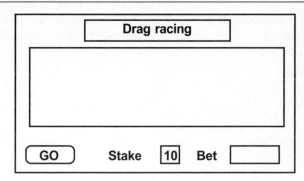

Figure 3.3 Rough design for the Drag Racing game

Before applications such as Visual Basic were available, this interface would have taken many weeks to create but with judicious use of the AWT, the time can now be reduced to minutes. We have already used one Java package, **java.io**, in order to write to the screen, but this program requires us to build a Windows-type interface. The package we require to do this is provided in **java.awt**. The first line in the example imports the package, allowing us to use library methods to build the interface.

We will be looking at the AWT in detail in a later chapter, so some of the code in the example may seem obscure. Briefly, we are using inheritance to give us access to the class **Frame**, which encapsulates a top-level application window. We are implementing the ActionListener and ItemListener interfaces to deal with events related to making a choice and clicking the button. We use a container class, **Panel**, which is also provided by the AWT to hold our components. We can also use a **LayoutManager** to organize the components on the panel.

```
import java.awt.*;
import java.awt.event.*;

public class Bets extends Frame implements ActionListener,
ItemListener
{
    private Choice numbers;
    // gives us a pull-down menu to list the numbers
```

```java
private TextField bet;          // holds the actual bet
private Button b;               // gives us a button to click on
public Bets( )                  //construct the object
{
   numbers = new Choice( );
   // initialize the pull-down menu
   // tie event to the itemStateChanged method
   numbers.addItemListener(this);
   numbers.addItem("1");
   numbers.addItem("2");
   numbers.addItem("3");
   numbers.addItem("4");
   numbers.addItem("5");

   bet = new TextField(2);
   // initialize a Text Field to hold 2 digits
   b = new Button("GO");  // initialize a button
   // tie button event to the actionPerformed method
   b.addActionListener(this);
   Panel p = new Panel( );
   // initialize a panel to put things on
   p.setLayout(new FlowLayout( ));
   // get a layout manager
   p.add(b); // add the button to the panel
   p.add(new Label("Stake"));
   p.add(numbers);
   p.add(new Label("Bet"));
   p.add(bet);
   add("South", p);
   // add the panel and all its components at base

   // add method to handle closing the window
   // see Event Handling for more on this style of handler
   this.addWindowListener(new WindowAdapter(){
      public void windowClosing(WindowEvent e)
      {
         System.exit(0);
      }
   });
}
```

```java
// we need a method to look after our choices
public void actionPerformed(ActionEvent e)
{
   String s = e.getActionCommand();

   if (s.equals("GO"))
   {
      start( );
   }
}

public void itemStateChanged(ItemEvent e)
{
   String result= null;
   result = Integer.toString(numbers.getSelectedIndex( )+1);
   bet.setText(result);
}

public void start( )
{
   //Insert code here to start race
   System.out.println("GO");
}

public static void main(String[] args)
{
   Frame f = new Bets( ); //declare and initialize a Frame
   f.setSize(300, 100);       // how big is it?
   f.show( );                 // wheel it on screen!
}

} // end class definition
```

The program, when run, will produce the interface shown in Figure 3.4.

Figure 3.4 Simple interface created from AWT components

The point of this exercise is twofold: to introduce a game that we shall develop at various stages throughout the book and to demonstrate the *use* of other objects in a programmer-defined class. Every time you see the keyword **new** used in the example code we are instantiating an object of a predefined class. Every component of this interface is found in the Java AWT. We can use these objects by importing the package into the program with the statement:

```
import java.awt..*;
```

at the top of the program.

Golden rule of programming – always check the Java documentation to see if there is anything available that will save you from doing any real work!

3.5 Building your own classes

In this section we will look at the process of designing our own classes, the decisions we make about what responsibilities a class should have, and how it will interact with other classes to give us a fully functioning program.

The example application we will examine is a mathematical calculator. The first thing to look at when designing classes is the verbal description of what the system is composed of. This should give us a first clue as to the identity of some of our classes.

- ◆ System: Calculator
- ◆ Components: Display
                         Keypad
- ◆ Functionality: Mathematics – Add
                                           – Subtract
                                           – Multiply
                                           – Divide
                                           – Cancel

Figure 3.5 A calculator user interface

There are two obvious candidates for classes here: *Display* and *Keypad*. If we can create a generic display and a generic keypad, we can use them again for other programs – these are components in the truest sense of the word. It is obvious that there is no inheritance relationship here, nor is there a compositional relationship, yet it is equally obvious that these objects must know about one another in order to work together.

So we have two classes and two problems – how do the classes communicate? and where does the maths get processed?

The first question is the easiest one to answer. We can pass an object as a parameter to the initialization method of a class; once it knows about the object it can send it messages. The second question is a little more complicated. We know that the keypad is a part of the overall graphical user interface, and we know that the mathematics will be done as a result of the keys being pressed. Why don't we bundle the mathematics with the keyboard? The answer is that if we were designing an applet, we probably would, but because we are designing an application, and because our company has also received orders for a set of burglar alarm interfaces, we would prefer to separate the functionality from the interface if possible.

To solve this problem we need to borrow a procedure from the realm of human–computer interaction (HCI). This procedure is called *task analysis* and is concerned with isolating the components of a task in order that we can understand it better and build successful computer interfaces.

Let's begin by examining the sequence of events that occur when we use a calculator.

❶   Enter a number

❷   Check that the number is displayed correctly

❸   If it is, enter an operator
       Else If it isn't press cancel and return to 1

❹   Enter a second number

❺   Check that it is displayed correctly

❻   If it is, enter an equals sign

❼   Read the result from the display

This sequence actually gives us four clear indications of subtasks:

- Entering a number
- Cancelling a number
- Entering an operator
- Entering an equals sign

In each of the first two subtasks, the display is used as a value holder – this may seem obvious, but will be significant later.

Let's look again at the subtask entering an operator. The number is on the screen, we check that it is the number we intended to type in and we press an operator button, or cancel it. If we cancel it, we don't need to store it anywhere; if we press an operator button, we do.

Do generic keypads have operator buttons?

If we separate the keypad from the operator pad we will have a truly generic keypad, which we could extend to become a burglar alarm pad. The keypad need only know about the display. Its area of responsibility is simply to write numbers onto a display, read numbers from it and cancel the wrong numbers.

The operators on the other hand define the mathematics. We can attach the mathematics to the operators, thus giving us a class that we can easily extend to give the calculator extra functionality. So we now have the possibility of using three classes to provide the GUI components and the functionality; **Display**, **Keypad** and **Maths**. We will also need a class to contain these components, one that we might call **Calculator**.

Let's look at the responsibilities of each class, and try to work out the methods they will need to be provided with.

The class **Calculator** merely needs to declare instances of the other classes and to provide the window in which the components will sit. It will also need to provide a handler for events occurring to that window. A skeleton definition would include:

```
public class Calculator extends Frame
{
   // Construct object here
   public Calculator( )
   {
      // Initialize objects and place on default panel
   }

   public static void main(String[] args)
   {
      // Display top level window
   }
}
```

Now let's examine our class **Display**. This class needs to furnish a text field, and the ability to read and write data to and from it.

```
class Display extends Panel
{
   // construct class
   public Display( )
   {
      // initialize object and place on panel
   }

   public void write(String s)
   {
      // write data in the form of a string to the textfield
   }
```

```
    public String read()
    {
        // read data from the textfield
    }
}
```

That is as much as we need for the **Display** class; there is no data processing attached. What is significant is the fact that text fields can only read and write strings. This means that we have to think of a way of converting a number to a string and back again, if we are to do any mathematics in the **Maths** class.

Before we go to the **Maths** class, we still have one simple class to create, the **Keypad**:

```
class Keypad extends Panel implements ActionListener
{
    Display monitor;
    // create instance variable so we can access it later
    public Keypad(Display myMonitor)
    // Keypad needs to know about Display
    {
        monitor = myMonitor; // initialize instance variable
        Panel p = new Panel( );
        // arrange a grid of 15 cells to hold buttons
        p.setLayout(new GridLayout(5,3));

        // Use loop to create buttons
        String[]buttonLabels={"0","1","2","3","4","5","6","7",
            "8", "9" ,".", "", "", "", "C"};
        Button[] buttons = new Button[15];
        for (int i = 0; i<=14; i++)
            {
            buttons[i] = new Button(buttonLabels[i]);
            buttons[i].addActionListener(this);
            p.add(buttons[i]);
            }
        add("Center",p);
    } // end constructor

    public void actionPerformed(ActionEvent e)
```

```
    {
        /* switch will take a char, not a string. Happily we can
        use a method from the string object to get the first
        (and only) char.*/
        char c = e.getActionCommand( ).charAt(0);
        switch(c)
        {
            case '0':
            case '1':
            case '2':
            case '3':
            case '4':
            case '5':
            case '6':
            case '7':
            case '8':
            case '9':
            case '.':
            /* All we need to do here is to read the display and
        add the latest input to it.*/
            monitor.write(monitor.read( ) + c);
            break;

            case 'C':
            // overwrite the wrong number with a blank
            monitor.write("");
            break;
        } // end switch
    } // end method
} // end class definition
```

Now we can turn our attention to the **Maths** class, the object that actually does the processing. The **Maths** object needs to know about the **Monitor** object, but since we are using the TextField as a holder for our figures, it doesn't need to know directly about the **Keypad**.

```
class Maths extends Panel implements ActionListener
{
    Display monitor;

    private double num1, num2, result;
    private char operand;
```

```java
public Maths(Display myMonitor)
{
    /* sets up the operator keys and copies myMonitor to
    monitor, this block works in the same way as the
    numeric keypad */
}

public void actionPerformed(ActionEvent e)
{
    char c = e.getActionCommand().charAt(0);
    switch (c)
    {
        case '+':
        case '*':
        case '-':
        case '/':
        /* At this point we assume that the number is correct, so
    the consequence of pressing an operand is to place the
    number into our private variable, using another library
    routine to convert the string from monitor into a double. */
        num1 = Double.valueOf(monitor.read( )).doubleValue( );
    // we also need to record the operator.....
        operand = c;
    // ....and clear the textField.
        monitor.write("");
        break;

        case '=':
        num2 = Double.valueOf(monitor.read( )).doubleValue( );
    // do the maths by calling a class method sum( )
        result = sum(num1, num2, operand);
    // write the answer to the display
        monitor.write(String.valueOf(result));
    }
}

    // And this is how the maths are done!
    public double sum(double x, double y, char z)
    {
        // initialize a variable to hold the answer
        double answer = 0;
```

```
        if (z == '+') answer = x + y;
        else if (z == '-') answer = x - y;
        else if (z == '*') answer = x * y;
        else if (z == '/') answer = x / y;
        return answer;
    }
} // end class
```

That is a bare bones implementation of our four classes. This is not the only way to implement a calculator, but it is reasonably economical and once the classes have been designed and we are clear about which classes need to send messages to each other then the implementation is simple. Your task now is to fill in the missing code from the class descriptions. Alternatively the complete code listing is provided below.

```
import java.awt.*;
import java.awt.event.*;

public class Calculator extends Frame
{
    private Display out;
    private Keypad in;
    private Maths sums;

    public Calculator( )
    {
        setLayout(new BorderLayout( ));

        out = new Display( );
        sums = new Maths(out);
        in = new Keypad(out);

        add("North", out);
        add("Center", in);
        add("East", sums);
        this.addWindowListener(new WindowAdapter(){
            public void windowClosing(WindowEvent e)
            {
                System.exit(0);
            }
        });
    }
```

```java
    public static void main(String[] args)
    {
       Frame f = new Calculator( );
       f.setSize(100, 200);
       f.show( );
    }
}

class Display extends Panel
{
    private TextField show;

    public Display( )
    {
       show = new TextField(10);
       Panel p = new Panel( );
       p.add(show);
       add ("Center", p);
    }

    public void write(String s)
    {
       show.setText(s);
    }

    public String read()
    {
       return show.getText();
    }
}

class Keypad extends Panel implements ActionListener
{
    private Display monitor;

    public Keypad(Display myMonitor)
    {
       monitor = myMonitor;
       Panel p = new Panel();
       p.setLayout(new GridLayout(5,3));
```

```java
      String[] buttonLabels={"0","1","2","3","4","5","6","7",
        "8","9",".","","","","C"}; // one line in source code
      Button[] buttons = new Button[15];
      for (int i = 0; i<=14; i++)
         {
            buttons[i] = new Button(buttonLabels[i]);
            buttons[i].addActionListener(this);
            p.add(buttons[i]);
         }
      add("Center", p);
   }

   public void actionPerformed(ActionEvent e)
   {
      char c = e.getActionCommand().charAt(0);
      switch(c)
      {
         case '0':
         case '1':
         case '2':
         case '3':
         case '4':
         case '5':
         case '6':
         case '7':
         case '8':
         case '9':
         case '.':
         monitor.write(monitor.read( ) + c);
         break;

         case 'C':
         monitor.write("");
         break;
      }
   }
}

class Maths extends Panel implements ActionListener
{
```

```java
private Display monitor;
private double num1, num2, result;
private char operand;
public Maths(Display myMonitor )
{
   monitor = myMonitor;
   Panel p = new Panel();
   p.setLayout(new GridLayout(5,1));
   String[] buttonLabels={"+","-","*","/","="};
   Button[] buttons = new Button[5];
   for (int i = 0; i<=4; i++)
      {
         buttons[i] = new Button(buttonLabels[i]);
         buttons[i].addActionListener(this);
         p.add(buttons[i]);
      }
   add("North",p);
}

public void actionPerformed(ActionEvent e)
{
   char c = e.getActionCommand().charAt(0);
   switch (c)
   {
      case '+':
      case '*':
      case '-':
      case '/':
      num1 = Double.valueOf(monitor.read( )).doubleValue( );
      operand = c;

      monitor.write("");
      break;

      case '=':
      num2 = Double.valueOf(monitor.read( )).doubleValue( );
      result = sum(num1, num2, operand);
      monitor.write(String.valueOf(result));
   }
}
```

```
public double sum(double x, double y, char z )
{
    double answer = 0;
    if (z == '+') answer = x + y;
    else if (z == '-') answer = x - y;
    else if (z == '*') answer = x * y;
    else if (z == '/') answer = x / y;
    return answer;
}
}
```

SUMMARY

✓ In this chapter we have covered classes and objects, we have seen the three relationships that classes can have (use, composition and inheritance) and we have examined the issues surrounding visibility of data and methods used in classes.

✓ We have seen how messages can be sent to classes from other classes and we have been through the design cycle for a simple object-oriented calculator.

✓ We have also looked briefly at the packages that are part of the Java API and we have learnt that life is too short to reinvent the wheel!

Exercises

❶ Design, using inheritance, a class structure to hold details of all employees in a company.

❷ Write a program to implement a burglar alarm, using the classes supplied with the calculator program. Your program should take input from a numerical keypad and check it against a known four-figure sequence. You should provide methods for the user to change the keycode and to display an "ALARM" message when the code is entered wrongly.

❸   Write a class called currentAccount that includes methods to deposit and withdraw money and to inspect the balance. Make three instances of this class called Fred, Jane and Tom. Initialize them all with the same amount of money and withdraw different amounts from each account. Get the balance printed to the screen. What can you deduce from this exercise about the object in the computer's memory?

4 | APPLETS

AIMS OF THIS CHAPTER

The aim of this chapter is to start creating some real-life programs written to the Java2 specification, using the **java.swing** classes and to display them in a web browser. In the course of this chapter we will do more work with methods, learn how to pass values from one method to another and how to put a finished applet into a web page using HTML tags. We will then move onto more advanced applets featuring simple animation and we will see how we can make our applets interactive.

4.1 The difference between applets and applications

An *application* is a computer program that is installed on a network or personal computer and run from a command line or by clicking on an icon. The code for that program is resident on the computer or network responsible for running it. Applications are able to read and write files, print and have access to the hard drive and operating system of the computer that they are running on.

An *applet* is a program that runs within a Java-enabled web browser such as Internet Explorer or Netscape. Usually, an applet will be resident on a remote server, and is called from within a web page written in HTML. Because there is no way of knowing what applets are contained within a web page, applets are not allowed to have access to the hard drive of a computer for security reasons. This means that an applet cannot invoke any other program, cannot directly save a file and cannot print. There are effectively two layers of protection from applets: firstly in the language itself (it is not possible to use certain features) and secondly Java-enabled browsers impose their own restrictions on applets.

Inevitably, there are differences in the way that Netscape and Internet Explorer handle applets. These are hardly documented and therefore unpredictable. For this reason, it is essential to check that an applet does perform in the browser, in a networked environment (load the file from your ISP, not from the local hard disk), before unleashing it onto the Internet.

An applet in Java2 is derived from (extends, inherits) the **JApplet** class, which is part of the **javax.swing** package. The **JApplet** class is itself a sub-class of **java.applet.Applet** so it provides a top-level panel for us to arrange GUI components on.

4.2 A first applet

For a first applet, we will do a multimedia version of the old favourite, Hello World. This applet will display a picture instead of some text. To accomplish this, you will need a picture in .GIF. or .JPEG format. It is useful to have a graphics workshop of some kind to look after file conversion. There are two that come very highly recommended, PaintShop Pro *(http://www.jasc.com/)* which is responsible for the images in this book and Graphic Workshop for Windows *(http://www.mindworkshop.com/alchemy/alchemy.html)*. Both of these can be downloaded from the Internet.

To create an applet, we extend (make a sub-class of) **javax.swing.JApplet**. This class inherits from **java.applet.Applet** a number of methods that are called automatically by the web browser – **init( )** which initializes the applet, **destroy( )** which frees system resources when the applet is stopped, **start( )** which kicks off the real action of the applet, and **stop( )** which pauses the applet's execution. As Applet is subclassed from **Component** – via **Container** and **Panel** – the **Component** method **paint( )** can be used to bring graphic images to the screen. We would normally override at least the **init( )** method, because this is the method that initializes all the variables and objects that the applet requires.

Overriding a method means supplying a body to the method which is different from the one provided by the Java library – or by the original programmer. Essentially it gives us a means of customizing a class that is provided with a very basic behaviour pattern. The example applet simply brings a graphic to the screen.

```java
import java.awt.*;
// we need the awt to use the Image class
import javax.swing.*;

public class helloApplet extends JApplet
{
   Image image;
   // declare the picture, to be stored as an object of type Image

   public void init( )
   {
      /*  The getImage function takes a URL and a filename as
       *  parameters. If we keep the image in the same
       *  directory as the class file, we need not supply a path. */
      image = getImage(getDocumentBase( ), "Jimmy.gif");
   }

   public void paint(Graphics g)
   {
      /* We use an awt graphics object to render the
       * image at position 1,1 */
      g.drawImage(image, 1, 1, this);
   }
}
```

The first thing you will notice about this code is that there is no **public static void main( )** statement. This is replaced in an applet by the **init( )** method, which initializes the applet – i.e. it sets up the environment so that the processing can take place. The **paint( )** method is called automatically. You can check that a method is being called very easily, and this is an excellent way to debug programmes that are not working in the intended way – add a line to the **import** section:

```java
import java.io.*;
```

This allows you to print to a DOS window while the applet is running in the AppletViewer. If you now add the line

```
System.out.println("Paint Method Called");
```

to the beginning of the **paint( )** method's body, the message will be printed out in the DOS window as soon as the computer executes that line. You can use this technique to check the value of variables at various stages in your program if you are getting unexpected results:

```
System.out.println("My variable x is: " + x +" at this point in
    the program")
```

Within init( ), the line

```
image = getImage(getDocumentBase( ), "Jimmy.gif");
```

uses the **getImage( )** method of the **Image** class in order to find the actual picture. The method takes a URL and a filename as arguments – here we are using the **getDocumentBase( )** method from **Applet** to get the location of the web page containing the applet. If we keep the picture in the same directory as the class file, then we can refer to it directly.

The **paint( )** method renders the contents of **image** to the screen, by using the **drawImage( )** method from **Graphics**. **paint(Graphics g)** gives us access to the **Graphics** methods.

```
g.drawImage(image, 0, 0, this);
```

drawImage( ) takes four parameters: a reference to the picture to be drawn, x and y coordinates to position the picture within the applet area and a reference to an ImageObserver interface. This relays information about the status of the image to our program.

Before we can run this class, we need to create an HTML setting for it.

4.3 Applets and HTML

Using the text editor, create a file called **Hello.html**, and save it to the same directory as your class and image. The file should contain the following text:

```
<HTML>
<BODY>
<APPLET CODE = "helloApplet.class" WIDTH =150 HEIGHT=150>
</APPLET>
```

This is the first applet in Teach Yourself Java
```
</BODY>
</HTML>
```

Having saved this file, you can view your applet by typing:

```
appletviewer Hello.html
```

at the command prompt.

You will probably find that it takes a second or two to render the image. We have used the Attributes WIDTH and HEIGHT, to tell the browser how much room to allow for the applet.

```
<HTML>
<HEAD>
<TITLE>Here's Johnny!</TITLE>
<BODY BGCOLOR= "LIGHTBLUE">
<H3> Wrapping Text</H3>
The following applet is meant to illustrate the ability of HTML to
display applets within a prescribed area, keeping a set margin
between the applet and the text.
<APPLET CODE = "helloApplet.class" WIDTH =150 HEIGHT=250
    ALIGN = LEFT VSPACE = 10 HSPACE=10>
</APPLET>
```

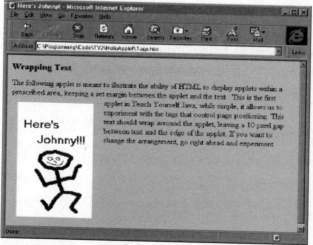

Figure 4.1 Displaying an Applet with text

This is the first applet in Teach Yourself Java, while simple, it allows us to experiment with the tags that control page positioning. This text should wrap around the applet, leaving a 10 pixel gap between text and the edge of the applet. If you want to change the arrangement, go right ahead and experiment.

```
</BODY>
</HTML>
```

These are the other tags available with ALIGN:

LEFT	Applet to left of page
RIGHT	Applet to right of page
BOTTOM	Bottom of applet in line with bottom of current line of text
TOP	Bottom of applet to top of current line of text
TEXTTOP	Top of applet to top of current line
MIDDLE	Middle of applet to base of current line
ABSMIDDLE	Middle of applet to middle of current line
BASELINE	Bottom of applet to baseline of current line
ABSBOTTOM	Bottom of applet to bottom of current line

You can also use the **<APPLET>** tag to pass parameters to an applet. This can be useful when you want to use a different font, for example, to make the Applet stand out from the rest of the text:

```
<APPLET CODE = "NewFont.class" WIDTH = 150 HEIGHT = 150>
<PARAM NAME=font VALUE="Courier">
</APPLET>
```

This parameter can be passed to the paint( ) method of an applet by including the line

```
String fontChoice = getParameter("font");
```

then set the font with

```
Font f = new Font(fontChoice, Font.BOLD, 25);
g.setFont(f);
```

and use it

```
g.drawString("This Font is large and looks like a typewriter!");
```

4.4 Java2 Applets

All Java2 applets require a plug-in to run in the current generation of browsers (IE5, Netscape 4). The simplest way to arrange this is to alter the HTML code so that the browser will prompt the user to download the plug-in. Any HTML file using the APPLET tag can be converted automatically by the Sun HTML Converter, which is available free from: **http://java.sun.com/products/plugin/**

We have just seen how we can put graphics into pages. Now we will look at text and fields.

The applet we are going to write is a simple temperature converter. The applet will contain two fields (JTextField), two text labels (JLabel) describing them and a Button (JButton) to trigger the conversion.

Figure 4.2 Centigrade/ fahrenheit conversion applet

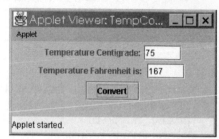

The first thing to know about these components is that they are classes belonging to the **javax.swing** package, so we need a line at the beginning of the program to import **javax.swing.*;** . **JTextField** represents characters as text in a field. All characters (including numbers) are treated as text if they are displayed in a field. This means that we have to explicitly convert them in both directions. Fortunately Java supplies us with library routines to do this.

```
Integer.parseInt(JTextFieldName.getText( ));
```

reads text and converts it to an integer value, and

```
JTextFieldName.setText(Integer.toString(f));
```

places an integer *f* into a TextField as a piece of text.

We need the compulsory **init( )** method to put the text and fields on the screen, an **actionPerformed( )** method to read text from the centigrade field and write it to the fahrenheit field and a **calc( )** method to do the conversion.

We need to declare all our variables at the top of the program before we write any code, so for this program we need two objects of type **JTextField**, two objects of type **JLabel** to hold the description or instructions, one **JButton** and three integers (two to hold the centigrade and fahrenheit values and one to hold the result after the calculation has been done).

The first part of the program will look like this:

```
import java.awt.*;
// We need a Container to place components on
import java.awt.event.*;
//We need events to be triggered by the Button
import javax.swing.*; // The J..components

public class TempCon extends JApplet implements
   ActionListener
{
   private JLabel CentLabel, FarLabel;
   private JTextField Centin, Farout;
   private JButton b;
   private int f, c, answer;

   public void init( )
   {
      CentLabel = new JLabel("Temperature Centigrade: ");
      Centin = new JTextField(5);

      FarLabel = new JLabel("Temperature Fahrenheit is: ");
      Farout = new JTextField(5);

      b = new JButton("Convert");
      b.addActionListener(this);

      Container c = getContentPane( ); // get context for drawing
      c.setLayout(new FlowLayout( )); // set Layout manager for c
      c.add(CentLabel); // add components to c
      c.add(Centin);
```

```
        c.add(FarLabel);
        c.add(Farout);
    }
```

Notice that after we have declared that we are going to use these **JLabel** and **JTextField** classes, we have to explicitly instantiate them in the **init( )** method. When we instantiate the objects, we can give them some information. The **JLabel** object needs to know the text, which is passed to it as a String and therefore needs to be contained within quotation marks. The **JTextField** needs to know how much text is expected to display, so we give it an integer argument enumerating the number of characters. After we have done this, we add the objects to the applet.

The next problem is how to deal with the input. For this, we will use an event handling method called **actionPerformed( )**. This method takes an *ActionEvent* as an argument. In this case the event is caused by the user hitting the 'Convert' button on the applet after they have entered the number. All we need to do is supply code to handle this event.

When we receive notification of the event, we need to read the text from the **JTextField**, convert it to a number, call our **calc( )** method to perform some number crunching on it and write the result back to the screen, as text:

```
public void actionPerformed(ActionEvent e)
{
    c = Integer.parseInt(Centin.getText( ));
    f = calc(c);
    Farout.setText(Integer.toString(f));
}
```

The last thing we should examine is the **calc( )** method:

```
public int calc(int x)
{
    answer=(((9 * x)/5) + 32);
    return answer;
}
```

The first line tells us that this is a public method, that it returns an integer value and that it takes an integer as an argument. The body of the code consists of the algorithm for converting centigrade into fahrenheit. Notice that in the method header the argument is specified as **integer** x, not **c**. This is because we are describing a type of variable, not a specific instance of one. When the method is called as **f = calc(c)** the compiler checks that **c** is an integer; similarly the return type must match the receiver **f**.

Here is the complete code:

```
import java.awt.*;
import java.awt.event.*;
import javax.swing.*;

public class TempCon extends JApplet implements
    ActionListener
{
    private JLabel CentLabel, FarLabel;
    private JTextField Centin, Farout;
    private JButton b;
    private int f, c, answer;

    public void init( )
    {
        CentLabel = new JLabel("Temperature Centigrade: ");
        Centin = new JTextField(5);

        FarLabel = new JLabel("Temperature Fahrenheit is: ");
        Farout = new JTextField(5);

        b = new JButton("Convert");
        b.addActionListener(this);

        Container c = getContentPane();
        c.setLayout(new FlowLayout());

        c.add(CentLabel);
        c.add(Centin);
        c.add(FarLabel);
        c.add(Farout);
        c.add(b);
    }

    public void actionPerformed(ActionEvent e)
```

```
    {
        c = Integer.parseInt(Centin.getText( ));
        f = calc(c);
        Farout.setText(Integer.toString(f));
    }
    public int calc(int x)
    {
        answer=(((9 * x)/5) + 32);
        return answer;
    }

} // end class definition
```

4.5 An interactive applet

The magic ingredient that Java offers to web designers is *interactivity*. For our next applet we will return to the racing game, and design a way of placing bets on the outcome of the race. The rules are quite straight-forward: the user starts with a pot of money, say £100, and places a bet on the outcome of the race. If the chosen car wins, the game adds to the pot a sum equal to the bet. If the chosen car loses, the game keeps the bet. When the user has no more money left, or presses the QUIT but-ton, the game ends.

We have not written any animation code yet – that will be coming up in the next chapter – so we will place our bets on the outcome of a ran-domly generated number between 1 and 4. The user can choose a number: if the computer's choice matches the number, the user wins.

The first thing to do is to declare the instance variables. We need inte-ger storage to hold the bet, the amount of money we have left in the pot, the amount of money the house has left (the bank) and the actual result of the race. We also need to declare the objects we are importing from swing, so every **JTextField**, **JLabel** and **JButton** will be de-clared here.

```
import java.awt.*;
import java.awt.event.*;
import java.util.*;
import javax.swing.*;
```

```java
public class Betting extends JApplet implements ActionListener
{
    private int bet, pot, bank, car, result;
    private JLabel betLabel, potLabel, bankLabel, carLabel;
    private JTextField betField, carField, potField, bankField,
        winnerField;
    private JButton goButton;

    public void init( )
    {

    }
}
```

We now need to fill in the public method **init( )**, so that everything shows up on the screen.

```java
public void init( )
    {
        betLabel = new JLabel("Enter Bet");
        carLabel = new JLabel("Choose Car");
        potLabel = new JLabel("Pot");
        bankLabel = new JLabel("Bank");

        betField = new JTextField(5);
        carField = new JTextField(2);
        potField = new JTextField(5);
        bankField = new JTextField(7);
        winnerField = new JTextField(20);

        potField.setEditable(false);
        bankField.setEditable(false);

        goButton = new JButton("Start Race");
        goButton.addActionListener(this);

        Container c = getContentPane();
        c.setLayout(new FlowLayout());

        c.add(goButton);
        c.add(betLabel);
        c.add(betField);
        c.add(carLabel);
```

```
        c.add(carField);
        c.add(potLabel);
        c.add(potField);
        c.add(bankLabel);
        c.add(bankField);
        c.add(winnerField);

        betField.setText("");
        potField.setText("100");
        bankField.setText("1000");
    }
```

Now that we have an interface, we need to know how to play the game. Remember at this point that the idea is to add this interface to a much larger program, so we need to make it as generic as possible.

The methods we will need are an event-handling method – **ActionPeformed( )** – to control the race via a push button, a method to give us a result – we will call this **race( )** (when we implement the game proper, this method will be replaced). The important thing is that **race( )** should return an integer, as that will give us something to compare with our predicted winner. We will need to check if we have won or not, so a method called **isWinner( )**, taking the actual result and comparing it with our prediction, will return a Boolean value true or false. Using this will be the **actionPerformed( )** method, which will read in the data, set the game off, wait for the result to be returned and administer winnings or, more likely, losses. The first thing to look at is our race method. In this context, all **race( )** needs to do is to return a randomly chosen number, restricted to a choice of 4 – we can do this by using the **Math.random( )** method from **java.util**, a technique that may come in useful later.

```
    public int Race( )
    {
        int z;
        z = 1 + (int) (Math.random( ) * 4);
        return z;
    }
```

Math.random( ) returns a double between 0.0 and 1.0. Here we are casting the result to an integer and adding it to 1, as we do not have a car number 0. We multiply it by 4 in order to give us a range between 1 and 4.

Our method to determine the winner is equally simple:

```
public boolean isWinner(int x, int y)
{
    if (x == y)
    return true;
    else
    return false;
}
```

When called, we give it the result of the race and our prediction as parameters and simply compare the two.

The **actionPerformed( )** method will provide the logic and control the game. To define this method, we can analyze the task of playing the game. Remembering that the game may be played several times by one user, the first thing to do is to clear the text from the winnerField. Now, for the sake of simplicity, we store the bets and state of our finances in the appropriate variables by converting the text values to integers as we did with the calculator.

Next we get the result of the race by calling **Race( )**, and print it out in the textField to avoid arguments later! All that remains is to administer the money, by subtracting the bet from the pot and adding it to the bank if we have lost, or vice versa in the unusual event that we win.

```
public void actionPerformed(ActionEvent e)
{
    winnerField.setText("");
    bet = Integer.parseInt(betField.getText( ));
    pot = Integer.parseInt(potField.getText( ));
    bank = Integer.parseInt(bankField.getText( ));
    car = Integer.parseInt(carField.getText( ));

    result = Race( );
    winnerField.setText("Winner is " + Integer.toString(result));

    if (isWinner(car, result) == true)
    {
```

```
      pot = pot + bet;
      potField.setText(Integer.toString(pot));
      bank = bank - bet;
      bankField.setText(Integer.toString(bank));
   }
   else
   {
      pot = pot - bet;
      potField.setText(Integer.toString(pot));
      bank = bank + bet;
      bankField.setText(Integer.toString(bank));
   }
}
```

Figure 4.3 shows the interface in Applet Viewer, and the code for the complete program is listed below. Try altering the program so that it checks to see if either the user or the bank has no money left and so that, instead of inputting the number of the car, we select it from a pull-down menu.

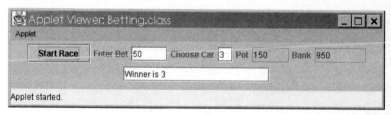

Figure 4.3 User interface for betting game

```
import java.awt.*;
import java.awt.event.*;
import java.util.*;
import javax.swing.*;

public class Betting extends JApplet implements ActionListener
{
   private int bet, pot, bank, car, result;
   private JLabel betLabel, potLabel, bankLabel, carLabel;
   private JTextField betField, carField, potField, bankField,
      winnerField;
   private JButton goButton;
```

```java
public void init( )
{
    betLabel = new JLabel("Enter Bet");
    carLabel = new JLabel("Choose Car");
    potLabel = new JLabel("Pot");
    bankLabel = new JLabel("Bank");

    betField = new JTextField(5);
    carField = new JTextField(2);
    potField = new JTextField(5);
    bankField = new JTextField(7);
    winnerField = new JTextField(20);
    potField.setEditable(false);
    bankField.setEditable(false);

    goButton = new JButton("Start Race");
    goButton.addActionListener(this);

    Container c = getContentPane();
    c.setLayout(new FlowLayout());

    c.add(goButton);
    c.add(betLabel);
    c.add(betField);
    c.add(carLabel);
    c.add(carField);
    c.add(potLabel);
    c.add(potField);
    c.add(bankLabel);
    c.add(bankField);
    c.add(winnerField);

    betField.setText("");
    potField.setText("100");
    bankField.setText("1000");
}

public int Race( )
{
    int z;

    z = 1 + (int) (Math.random() * 4);
```

```
      return z;
   }

   public boolean isWinner(int x, int y)
   {
      if (x == y)
         return true;
      else
         return false;
   }

   public void actionPerformed(ActionEvent e)
   {
      winnerField.setText("");
      bet = Integer.parseInt(betField.getText( ));
      pot = Integer.parseInt(potField.getText( ));
      bank = Integer.parseInt(bankField.getText( ));
      car = Integer.parseInt(carField.getText( ));

      result = Race( );
      winnerField.setText("Winner is " + Integer.toString(result));

      if (isWinner(car, result) == true)
      {
         pot = pot + bet;
         potField.setText(Integer.toString(pot));
         bank = bank - bet;
         bankField.setText(Integer.toString(bank));
      }
      else
      {
         pot = pot - bet;
         potField.setText(Integer.toString(pot));
         bank = bank + bet;
         bankField.setText(Integer.toString(bank));
      }
   } // end method definition

} // end class definition
```

4.6 Simple animation

As we have already seen, loading a graphic into an applet is not terribly hard. The next task is to try our hand at an animation. This will introduce us to several techniques that are used extensively in graphics programming. For this animation we are going to try to emulate a children's book style animation, where a figure is drawn with a slight difference on successive pages and the user flicks through the book in order to create the illusion of movement.

The first thing you need to do is to prepare 20 different small images. Start with one, and call it *filename*0.gif . The actual name is unimportant, but try to use something descriptive, and append a zero to the filename. Now alter the image very slightly and save it as *filename*1.gif. Keep doing this until you have 21 images, numbered 0–20. Save these images into the same directory as your class files.

Now we can start the programming part. This should be simple: in theory all we need to do is to run a loop that will increment the picture number and render it to the screen.

```java
import javax.swing.*;
import java.awt.*;

public class SimpleAnimation extends JApplet
{
    private Image images[ ];
    private int frames = 20;

    public void init( )
    {
        images = new Image[frames];

        for (int i = 0; i < frames; i++)
        {
            images[i] = getImage(getDocumentBase( ), "Smile" + i
                + ".gif");
        }
    }
```

```
public void paint(Graphics g)
{
    for (int i = 0; i < frames; i++)
    {
        g.drawImage(images[i], 1, 1, this);
    }
}
public void start( )
{
    repaint( );
}

}
```

4.7 Slide shows

To create a slide show, we will need to create a separate **thread of execution**. A thread is a path of execution through a program. This applet is not truly multi-threaded, but we need to set up a single different thread in order to slow the main program down. This is a very common use of threads – setting up timers to control the rate of execution of a program.

As you might recall from Chapter 3, we have a choice about how we implement a thread. We can use the **Thread** class, extend it to suit our purposes and compose our program using our improved version, or we can invoke the **Runnable** interface, which allows us to use a **run( )** method to control the applet. With applets this is the more common solution as it cuts down on the number of classes used and therefore on the number of http calls to the server.

Implementing an interface is a convenient way of borrowing the behaviour of an object without actually using inheritance. An *interface* is a collection of methods that we must implement if we choose to use this technique. **Runnable** includes just one method – **run( )** – which is automatically passed to the Thread class.

```
import javax.swing.*;
import java.awt.*;
```

```java
public class SimpleAnimation extends JApplet implements Runnable
{
    private Thread animate;  // declare a Thread
    private Image images[ ];
    private int frames = 20;
    private int count = 0;

    public void init( )
    {
        // load all the images
        images = new Image[frames];

        for (int i = 0; i < frames; i++)
        {
            images[i] = getImage(getDocumentBase( ), "Smile" + i
                + ".gif");
        }
    }

    public void paint(Graphics g)
    {
        g.drawImage(images[count++], 1, 1, this);
        if (count == frames)
            count = 0;
    }

    public void start( )
    {
        if (animate == null)
        {
            animate = new Thread(this);  // initialize a thread
            animate.start( );  // starts thread running - calls run( )
        }
    }

    public void stop( )
    {
        if (animate != null)
        {
            animate = null;  // free up resources
```

```
        }
    }

    public void run( )
    {
        while (isActive( ))  // while there is a live thread
        {
            try // loop through this sequence
            {
                repaint( );
                Thread.sleep(1000); // pause the thread 1 second
            }
            catch (InterruptedException e)
            {
            }

            animate = null;
        } // end while
    } // end method

  } // end class definition
```

When using threads, it is important to realize that the relationship between **start( )** and **run( )** is implicit – **run( )** is called automatically by
start( ). To stop a thread simply give it a null value, as in the example.

4.8 Converting an applet to an application

Simplistically, extend **JFrame** in place of **JApplet**, change the **init**
method to a constructor and provide a **main** method to create an
instance of the class.

If only it were that simple…

If you are using graphics in the applet, you will have to paint them onto
a **JPanel** and place the **JPanel** onto the **JFrame** – for an example of
this technique see Chapter 10. You will also have to set the size of the
display and use the **JFrame** method **setVisible(true)** to render the application to the screen.

SUMMARY

✓ In this chapter we have learnt the difference between applets and applications. We have written applets that display graphics and manipulate figures, and while doing this have looked in detail at the techniques covered in earlier chapters, putting them to use.

✓ We have looked at the use of multiple methods to break a task down into easy to code chunks, notably the use of the **calc( )** method in the temperature conversion program and **isWinner( )** in the betting game.

✓ In addition we have touched on areas that we will be covering in later chapters, most notably graphics and threads. We have demonstrated that a graphic file can be loaded from a remote server and displayed in the graphics context of an applet. We have also learnt how to set up a simple thread so that the main program can control the rate at which the calls to **paint( )** are made.

Exercises

❶ Rewrite the Bets program to include methods for preventing the user from betting more funds than are available.

❷ Add a function to return the square of a given number to the calculator program.

❸ Revise the slide show applet to include a pause button, which pauses at one click and releases on the second. (**Hint** – You will need to set a state for the button in the **actionPerformed( )** method.)

❹ Revise the slide show to pause on a single mouse click. You will need to consult the Java API or later chapters of this book in order to discover how to do this.

5 | SIMPLE GRAPHICS WITH JAVA2D

AIMS OF THIS CHAPTER

The aims of this chapter are to build up an understanding of how computers use coordinates on the screen to position components, to write programs that create graphics primitives using java.awt and java.awt.geom. and to gain an understanding of the role of paint( ), update( ) and repaint( ) methods in getting graphics to the screen. We will look at how the new Graphics2D class is related to the original Graphics and compare their use in programs performing similar functions.

We will examine colour, fonts and shapes and look at ways in which we might control the presentation of text within a screen.

5.1 A first graphics program

In this program, we will see how the computer uses x and y coordinates to position components on the screen.

A computer screen is composed of pixels and, depending on the resolution, is bounded by a known number of pixels. Typically a display will be set to 800×600 or 1280×1024 pixels. The top left-hand corner is given the coordinates 0, 0. The first coordinate gives the position on the x (horizontal) axis, the second the y (vertical) axis.

This application will draw a line, following the mouse around the screen, and print out the coordinates at the bottom of the window. *Inner classes* are also featured here for the first time – in this case, it is better to use an **Adapter** class to handle the events because implementing the **MouseMotionListener** interface would mean that we would have to supply every method specified by that interface. See Chapter 8 for more on event handling.

```java
import java.awt.*;
import javax.swing.*;
import java.awt.event.*;

public class Coordinates extends JFrame
{
    private int lastX, lastY;
    private Color myColor = Color.blue;
    private JLabel status;

    // set up background colour
    public Coordinates( )
    {
        status = new JLabel( );
        getContentPane( ).add(status, BorderLayout.SOUTH);
        addMouseListener(new MouseClickHandler());
        addMouseMotionListener(new MouseMotionHandler());
    }

    private class MouseClickHandler extends MouseAdapter
    {
        // catches the mouse event to get first coordinates
        public void mousePressed(MouseEvent e)
        {
            lastX = e.getX();
            lastY = e.getY();
        }
    }

    private class MouseMotionHandler extends MouseMotionAdapter
    {
        // draws a line from last coordinates to current ones
        public void mouseDragged(MouseEvent e)
        {
            Graphics g = getGraphics( );
            g.setColor(myColor);
```

```
            g.drawLine(lastX, lastY, e.getX(), e.getY());
            lastX = e.getX();
            lastY = e.getY();
            status.setText("(Mouse is at: "+ lastX + "," + lastY + ")");
        }
    }

    public static void main(String[] args)
    {
        JFrame f = new Coordinates();
        f.setSize(500, 500);
        f.show();
    }
}
```

This is an extremely basic drawing application. We get the first set of coordinates from the initial **mousePressed** event then, as we drag the mouse around the screen, the coordinates are constantly updated and joined together.

5.2 Fonts

Our next application will demonstrate drawing text to the screen, in different fonts, colours and sizes. As with previous class definitions, the first thing we do is to declare our data – here we are going to use a series of **String** objects which can be declared and initialized at one go. We are also going to call on the **awt.Font** class to give us some control over what the text will look like.

```
    import java.awt.*;
    import javax.swing.*;

    public class Fonts extends JFrame
    {
        private String s = "What are the details of this Font?";

        private Font f;

        public Fonts( )
        {
            setBackground(Color.black);
```

```
        f = new Font("TimesRoman", Font.ITALIC, 20);
    }
  }
```

We also define our **font** in the *constructor* method. A **Font** definition takes three arguments: a **String** describing the name of the **Font**, a call to the **Font** class to determine the presentation style (this is always done in capital letters: BOLD, ITALIC or PLAIN), and finally a point size integer which maps exactly onto the point sizes we are used to using in word processors. We could define further fonts thus:

```
    public Fonts( )
      {
          setBackground(Color.black);
          f1 = new Font("Helvetica", Font.ITALIC, 16);
          f2 = new Font("TimesRoman", Font.BOLD, 12);
          f3 = new Font("Courier", Font.PLAIN, 18);
      }
```

Now that we have set the application up, all that remains is to draw the text to the screen. This is done via a call to Graphics. In this case, because we are using different colours and fonts, we need three calls to Graphics for each line – one to set the colour, one to set the font and another to draw the string. The call to **Graphics.setColor** takes the colour constant available to Color as an argument, **Graphics.setFont** takes our pre-defined font style as an argument and **Graphics.drawString** takes the pre-defined **String** and the x and y coordinates that determine its position on the application.

```
    public void paint(Graphics g)
      {
          g.setColor(Color.red);
          g.setFont(f);
          g.drawString(s1, 20, 20);
      }
```

There are also graphics methods available to check what fonts are available, what font is being used and the size of the font being used. The application will demonstrate the use of these methods and the use of the **FontMetrics** class to get more detailed information about fonts.

The **FontMetrics** class gives us six methods for obtaining information about a font.

getFont( )	Returns a Font object.
getFontList( )	Returns a list of available fonts.
getAscent( )	Returns the height in points of the highest letter.
getDescent( )	Returns the depth the font requires below the baseline.
getLeading( )	Returns the leading – height above the letter, between lines.
getHeight( )	Returns the height of a font.

The **FontMetrics** class is not derived from **Font**; it is derived from **Object**. This means that when we use it, we use it with the current **Graphics** object rather than the current Font object.

```java
import java.awt.*;
import javax.swing.*;

public class Fonts extends JFrame
{
    private String s = "What are the details of this Font?";

    private Font f;

    public Fonts1( )
    {
        setBackground(Color.black);
        f = new Font("TimesRoman", Font.ITALIC, 20);
    }

    public void paint(Graphics g)
    {
        int style, size;
        String s1, s2, s3, s4, s5, s6, s7, name;

        g.setColor(Color.red);
        g.setFont(f);
        g.drawString(s, 20, 20);
```

```java
        s1 = f.getName( );  // retrieve name of Font
        /* retrieve style of Font – note that getStyle returns an int
         * value which we map onto a Font Style   */
        style = f.getStyle( );
        if (style == Font.PLAIN)
            s2 = "Plain";
        else if (style == Font.BOLD)
            s2 = "Bold";
        else if (style == Font.ITALIC)
            s2 = "Italic";
        else s2 = "";

        s3 = f.getSize( ) + " point ";  // retrieve size of Font

        g.drawString(s1, 20, 50);
        g.drawString(s2, 20, 70);
        g.drawString(s3, 20, 90);

        g.drawString("Font family is " + f.getFamily( ), 20, 110);

        int ascent = g.getFontMetrics( ).getAscent( );
        int descent = g.getFontMetrics( ).getDescent( );
        int height = g.getFontMetrics( ).getHeight( );
        int leading = g.getFontMetrics( ).getLeading( );

        s4 = "Ascent of Font = " + String.valueOf(ascent);
        s5 = "Descent of Font = " + String.valueOf(descent);
        s6 = "Height of Font = " + String.valueOf(height);
        s7 = "Leading of Font = " + String.valueOf(leading);

        g.drawString(s4, 20, 140);
        g.drawString(s5, 20, 170);
        g.drawString(s6, 20, 200);
        g.drawString(s7, 20, 230);
    }

    public static void main(String[] args)
    {
        JFrame f = new Fonts1();
        f.setSize(400, 400);
        f.show();
    }
}
```

These methods, in isolation, are fairly unspectacular. They are useful for animating text, in ways that will be demonstrated at the end of the chapter.

5.3 Colours

This section will make use of the **JColorChooser**, one of the additional widgets available in the Swing package. This widget allows the user to choose a colour from a swatch, and returns that colour to the calling program.

Colour is created from an RGB value. Java expresses RGB values as three integers with a range of 0–255. Each value controls the amount of red, green or blue that makes up the colour required. The methods associated with colour are defined in the Color class and include:

getRed( )	Returns the R value.
getGreen( )	Returns the Green value.
getBlue( )	Returns the Blue value.

In addition to these, there are methods to get and set the colour:

getColor( )	Returns a colour object representing the current colour.
setColor(Color c)	Sets the colour to be used by graphics objects

```java
import java.awt.*;
import javax.swing.*;
import java.awt.event.*;

public class Colour extends JFrame implements ActionListener
{
    private Color c1;
    private String s, s1, s2, s3;
    private JButton b;
    private Container c;

    public Colour( )
    {
        c = getContentPane();
        c.setLayout(new FlowLayout());
```

```java
      b = new JButton("Choose new Background Colour");
      b.addActionListener(this);
      c1 = Color.black;
      setBackground(c1);
      c.add(b);
   }

   public void actionPerformed(ActionEvent e)
   {
      c1 = JColorChooser.showDialog(this, "Choose new
         Background Colour", c1);
      if (c1 == null)
      c1 = Color.black;
      setBackground(c1);
      repaint();
   }

   public void update(Graphics g)
   {
      paint(g);
   }

   public void paint(Graphics g)
   {
      g.setColor(Color.red);
      s1 = String.valueOf(c1.getRed( ));
      s2 = String.valueOf(c1.getGreen( ));
      s3 = String.valueOf(c1.getBlue( ));

      g.drawString("Current background colour is RGB(" + s1 +
         "," + s2+ ","+ s3 + ")", 20, 170);
   }

   public static void main(String[] args)
   {
      JFrame f = new Colour();
      f.setSize(400, 400);
      f.show();
   }

} // end class definition
```

5.4 Shapes

The Java AWT provides a number of graphics primitives that can be
used to create basic shapes. These primitives can be used via methods
of the **Graphics** class. The first primitive is a line:

```java
import java.awt.*;
import javax.swing.*;

public class OldLine extends JFrame
{
   private Color c, bc;

   public OldLine( )
   {
      bc = Color.black;
      c = Color.white;
      setBackground(bc);
   }

   public void paint(Graphics g)
   {
      g.setColor(c);
      g.drawLine(20, 20, 100, 100);
   }

   public static void main(String[] args)
   {
      JFrame f = new OldLine();
      f.setSize(100, 100);
      f.show();
   }
}
```

This program simply makes the background black, sets the graphics
colour to white and draws a line from 20, 20 to 100, 100 using the
Graphics.drawLine( ) method. If we want to do anything more interesting with lines, we have to use rectangles with a bit of imagination.

Using Java2D, we can create a line just as easily. The main points to
notice are that we need to cast our graphics object to a Java2D graphics
object, which we import from **java.awt.geom** and that the line is itself

an object with its own constructors. The constructor used here simply sets the end points of the line.

```java
import javax.swing.*;
import java.awt.*;
import java.awt.geom.*;

public class NewLine extends JFrame
{
    private Color c , bc;

    public NewLine( )
    {
        bc = Color.black;
        c = Color.white;
        setBackground(bc);
    }

    public void paint(Graphics g)
    {
        Graphics2D g2 = (Graphics2D)g;
        Line2D line = new Line2D.Double(20, 20, 100, 100);
        g2.setPaint(Color.blue);
        g2.draw(line);
    }

    public static void main(String[] args)
    {
        JFrame f = new NewLine();
        f.setSize(100, 100);
        f.show();
    }
}
```

In this next example we can see how a line might be manipulated by providing a variable to move one of the point coordinates:

```java
import javax.swing.*;
import java.awt.*;
import java.awt.geom.*;

public class Lightning extends JFrame
{
```

```java
   private Color c , bc;
   private int numLines = 20;

   public Lightning( )
   {
      bc = Color.black;
      c = Color.white;
      setBackground(bc);
   }
   public void paint(Graphics g)
   {
      Graphics2D g2 = (Graphics2D)g;
      for (int i = 0; i <= numLines; i++)
      {
         Line2D line = new Line2D.Double(10, i, 100, 100);
         g2.setPaint(c);
         g2.draw(line);
      }
   }

   public static void main(String[] args)
   {
      JFrame f = new Lightning( );
      f.setSize(100, 100);
      f.show();
   }
}
```

In the following program, we will draw rectangles using the AWT graphics methods:

```
   drawRect(x, y, width, height)
   fillRect(x, y, width, height)
   draw3DRect(x, y, width, height, true/false)
   fill3DRect(x, y, width, height, true/false)
```

Notice the Boolean in the 3D Rectangle – *true* indicates that the rectangle should be raised, *false* indicates that the rectangle should be sunken,with a frame around it.

Figure 5.1
Drawing a rectangle

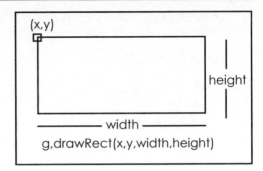

```java
import java.awt.*;
import javax.swing.*;

public class OldRectangle extends JFrame
{
   private Color c, c2,c3, bc;

   public OldRectangle( )
   {
      bc = Color.black;
      c = Color.white;
      c2 = Color.red;
      c3 = Color.pink;
      setBackground(bc);
   }

   public void paint(Graphics g)
   {
      // filled rectangle with a frame
      g.setColor(c2);
      g.drawRect(50, 50, 100, 50);
      g.fillRect(55, 55, 90, 40);

      // filled rectangle with 3D frame
      g.setColor(c);
      g.draw3DRect(110, 110, 80, 130, true);
      g.fill3DRect(112, 112, 76, 126, false);

      // Floating rectangle
      g.setColor(c3);
      g.draw3DRect(200, 200, 100, 150, false);
```

```
      g.fill3DRect(198, 198, 96, 146, true);
   }

   public static void main(String[] args)
   {
      JFrame f = new OldRectangle();
      f.setSize(600, 600);
      f.show();
   }
}
```

It is worth noting that Graphics2D extends Graphics; therefore anything that could be done with the graphics class can also be done with the Graphics2D class.

This is the paint method of the previous program, remodelled to use Graphics2D:

```
public void paint(Graphics g)
{
   Graphics2D g2 = (Graphics2D )g;

   Rectangle2D r = new Rectangle2D.Double(50, 50, 100, 50);
   g2.setPaint(c2); //new in Graphics2D
   g2.draw(r); // new in Graphics2D

   Rectangle2D r2 = new Rectangle2D.Double(55, 55, 90, 40);
   g2.fill(r2); // new in Graphics2D

   // filled rectangle with 3D frame
   g2.setColor(c); // graphics methods from here on!
   g2.draw3DRect(110, 110, 80, 130, true);
   g2.fill3DRect(112, 112, 76, 126, false);

   // Floating rectangle
   g2.setColor(c3);
   g2.draw3DRect(200, 200, 100, 150, false);
   g2.fill3DRect(198, 198, 96, 146, true);
}
```

We can use similar methods to draw rounded rectangles – again four parameters are required, and again they represent a starting point, a width and a height.

Here is the paint method of a program to draw rounded rectangles. The rest of the program is identical to **OldRectangle**.

```java
public void paint(Graphics g)
{
    g.setColor(c);
    // draw rounded rectangle
    g.drawRoundRect(20, 20, 50, 50, 10, 20);

    g.setColor(c2);
    // draw curvier rectangle
    g.fillRoundRect(100, 100, 80, 130, 50, 50);

    g.setColor(c2);
    // draw square
    g.drawRoundRect(200, 200, 100, 130, 0, 0);

    //draw circle
    g.fillRoundRect(300, 300, 80, 80, 80, 80);
}
```

You will notice that the method **drawRoundRect** takes two extra arguments. These dictate the height and width of the curved area at the corner.

Figure 5.2
A rounded rectangle

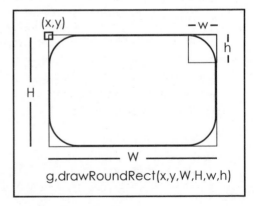

g,drawRoundRect(x,y,W,H,w,h)

Methods available to draw rounded rectangles are:

```
drawRoundRect(x, y, W, H, w, h)
fillRoundRect(x, y, W, H, w, h)
```

As we observed in the previous application, a curved rectangle can be
manipulated to form a circle by making the width and height of the
curved area equal to half the width and height of the rectangle. A separate method exists to draw ovals. To predict where an oval will be
drawn, imagine it is inside the smallest possible rectangle that would
enclose it. The starting point is the top left-hand corner of the rectangle, which is actually outside the oval. The oval only touches the sides
of the rectangle at the mid point.

Figure 5.3
Drawing an oval

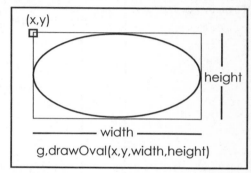

Methods available to draw ovals are:

```
drawOval(x, y, width, height)
fillOval(x, y, width, height)
```

Here is the paint method required to draw arcs. Notice that a filled arc
fills the 'slice' between the arc and the centre of the bounding rectangle.
An ordinary arc is also drawn relative to the rectangle's centre. To
illustrate this, the arc in the following program is drawn inside a rectangle which has the same starting point.

```
public void paint(Graphics g)
{
    g.setColor(c2);
    g.drawRect(100, 100, 150, 100);
    g.setColor(c);
    g.fillArc(100, 100, 150, 100, 35, -130);
}
```

Notice that an arc takes six arguments. These represent the starting
point, the width and height of the bounding rectangle, the starting angle measured from zero degrees at compass point east in an anticlock-

wise direction, and the angle of the arc, measured from the starting point to the end point. The minus sign in the last argument indicates that we want the arc to sweep in a clockwise direction.

Methods available to draw arcs are:

```
g.drawArc(x, y, w, h, start, finish);
g.fillArc(x, y, w, h, start, finish);
```

Figure 5.4
Drawing an arc

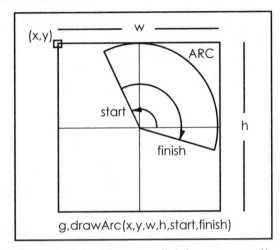

g,drawArc(x,y,w,h,start,finish)

Polygons may also be drawn in Java. These are slightly more complicated because their nature is not fixed. A polygon can have any number of sides, so our job is to define the points that make up the beginning and end of each side, and then join them together. The **drawPolygon** method takes two arrays of integers containing the *x* and *y* coordinates and a single integer declaring the number of sides as arguments. The last set of coordinates should be the same as the first set – if you want the polygon to be complete. Java does not assume that all polygons are closed, so your number of points should be one greater than the number of sides.

```
import javax.swing.*;
import java.awt.*;

public class TestPolygon extends JFrame
{
    private int xCoords[] = {30, 100, 250, 140, 30};
```

```java
    private int yCoords[] = {30, 100, 180, 75, 30};

    private Polygon p;

    public TestPolygon()
    {
        p = new Polygon(xCoords, yCoords, 5);
    }

    public void paint(Graphics g)
    {
        g.setColor(Color.green);
        g.drawPolygon(p);
    }

    public static void main(String[] args)
    {
        JFrame f = new TestPolygon();
        f.setSize(350, 350);
        f.show();
    }
}
```

This is not the only way to declare and draw a polygon. Another method allows us to add the points individually as pairs of x and y coordinates:

```java
    public TestPolygon( )
    {
        p = new Polygon( );

        p.addPoint(20, 20);
        p.addPoint(100, 100);
        p.addPoint(250, 180);
        p.addPoint(140, 75);
        p.addPoint(20, 20);
    }
```

Methods available to draw polygons are:

```java
    g.drawPolygon(p) //sketches the outline
    g.fillPolygon(p) // sketches the outline and fills it in
    g.drawPolygon(xCoords, yCoords, numPoints)
    g.fillPolygon(xCoords, yCoords, numPoints)
```

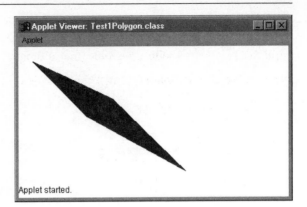

Applet Viewer: Test1Polygon.class

Figure 5.5
Drawing a
polygon

5.5 paint( ), repaint( ) and update( )

We have looked in some detail at ways of drawing text and images
onto an application. The methods **paint( )**, **repaint( )** and **update( )** all
belong to the Component class of the AWT. They take as an argument
an object of type Graphics, which represents the context in which the
application does its drawing. The Graphics class supplies the methods
that we have used in this chapter to draw text and images and to set the
paint mode.

The drawing reaches the screen via the **paint( )** method of **Component**.
However, when a window is open on a screen we cannot control what
happens to it. It may be resized by the user; another window may be
opened on top of it; it may be moved. These events are beyond our
control, yet the window remains intact. The reason for this is the **up-
date( )** method of Component. This method is called automatically
when any of these events occur – its default implementation is to erase
the background and call the **paint( )** method. As our drawing code is
usually in the **paint( )** method, this is adequate behaviour for most
circumstances. It may be necessary with some programs to override
the default implementation and provide a different sequence of actions
for **update( )**. For example, if we are rebuilding a static image, it is
obviously not necessary to erase the background, because it can be
used again.

Another rendering method associated with Component is **repaint( )**. This method in its default form sends a request to the AWT to call the **update( )** method as soon as possible (thus ultimately calling **paint( )**).

There are four ways that **repaint( )** can be called:

repaint( )	Calls update( ) asap.
repaint(*long* t)	Calls update( ) in *t* milliseconds
repaint(x, y, w, h)	Calls update( ) but repaints only the rectangle (x, y, w, h)
repaint(*long* t, x, y, w, h)	Calls update( ) and repaints the rectangle (x, y, w, h) in *t* milliseconds.

When using a **JPanel** as a 'canvas' to hold graphics, we use the **paintComponent( )** method instead of **paint( ).** This ensures that the component is rendered correctly on screen. See Chapter 10 for an example.

5.6 Graphics modes

Graphics modes dictate how graphics are drawn on the screen. If you alter one of the example programs to have the computer draw overlapping shapes, you will notice that the first shape is partially obscured by the second. This is the default graphics mode, known as *overwrite mode.*

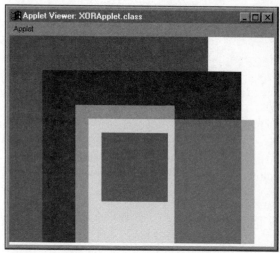

Figure 5.6
XOR mode
graphics

The other graphics mode is called *XOR*, and its effect is that all the overlapped shapes can still be seen. To invoke XOR mode, we use the Graphics method **setXORMode(Color c)**. The colour that is used as an argument to **setXORMode** dictates the colour of the overlapped area and where both shapes are of the same colour the overlapping area will be set to this colour. Where they are different colours, this colour is used to find a 'balancing' colour.

Here is the code used to generate the picture in Figure 5.6:

```java
import javax.swing.*;
import java.awt.*;

public class XORApp extends JFrame
{
    private Color c1, c2, c3, c4;

    public XORApp( )
    {
        c1 = Color.red;
        c2 = Color.blue;
        c3 = Color.green;
        c4 = Color.yellow;
    }

    public void paint(Graphics g)
    {
        g.setColor(c1);
        g.fillRect(0, 0, 300, 400);
        g.setColor(c2);
        g.fillRect(50, 50, 300, 400);
        g.setColor(c3);
        g.fillRect(100, 100, 150, 200);
        g.setXORMode(c4);
        g.fillRect(120, 120, 250, 300);
        g.setColor(c1);
        g.fillRect(140, 140, 100, 100);
    }

    public static void main(String[] args)
    {
```

```
        JFrame f = new XORApp();
        f.setSize(300, 300);
        f.show();
    }
}
```

Notice that the fourth overlapping rectangle has its mode set to XOR. The result of this is that the overlapping areas are represented in different colours. The last rectangle is painted in overwrite mode and therefore appears in its own colour, even though it overlaps another rectangle.

5.7 Graphics techniques

In this section, we will look at some common graphics techniques that are used to provide flicker-free rendering of animations to the screen. These techniques include the use of threads to slow an animation down, of **ImageObserver** to load images, of clipping to minimize the redrawn area and buffering to smooth the passage of pictures to the screen.

5.7.1 Threads

A *thread* refers to a sequence of operations forming a discrete task. In a multitasking operating system, we have an opportunity to organize concurrent processing of many tasks in order to increase the speed and efficiency of the program. Normally this is transparent to the user – it simply allows the computer to process some part of a program in the background, or to run multiple instances of the same class. The use of threads in programming is exactly analogous to multitasking in an operating system. It is a very useful technique in the writing of user interfaces, because we can convey to the user the impression that their input is being processed immediately by putting the user I/O in a separate thread.

The use of threads in Java is not restricted to graphics programs (it is used extensively in communications programming for example). However, the technique can be used to control animations very effectively.

The major problem with computer animation is that the progress of the animation has to be controlled by some sort of timer. If we use a simple looping structure, a modern processor will go through the loop so fast that the effect is lost. It takes considerably more processing power to paint a graphic to the screen than it does to read through a sequence of integers. The effect is that the count has progressed before the computer has had time to draw the picture. Using a thread we can slow the process down to a reasonable speed, thus allowing a smoother operation.

Let's examine the applet we used at the end of Chapter 4 to run a slide show. If we add some debugging code into it, so that we can see what's causing the problems, we should be able to solve them (extra code is shown in *italics*).

```java
import java.awt.*;
import java.io.*;
import javax.swing.*;

public class Smile extends JApplet implements Runnable
{
    private Thread animate; // declare a Thread
    private Image images[ ];
    private int frames = 20;
    private int count = 0;

    public void init( )
    {
        images = new Image[frames];
        for (int i = 0; i < frames; i++)
        {
            images[i] = getImage(getDocumentBase( ), "Smile" + i
                + ".gif");
        }
    }

    public void paint(Graphics g)
    {
        g.drawImage(images[count++], 1, 1, this);
        System.out.println(" painting image: " + count);
        if (count == frames)
            count = 0;
    }

    public void start( )
    {
```

```
        if (animate == null)
        {
          animate = new Thread( this ); // initialize a thread
          animate.start( );
          System.out.println("New Thread starting.....");
        }
      }

      public void run( )
      {
        while (isActive( ))
        {
          try
          {
            System.out.println("Thread calling paint");
            repaint( );
            Thread.sleep(1000 ); // pause the thread
          }
          catch (InterruptedException e)
          {
            System.out.println("Exception: "+ e.getMessage( ));
          }

        } // end while
      } // end method
    } // end class definition
```

Run this program and watch the Command window. The first thing to notice is that the thread starts on schedule. Next, we see that the computer runs through the whole list of pictures before we get a second call to paint. This is not what we expected to happen at all, the whole point of the thread was to increment one image at a time. Why should this be happening?

The answer is that our paint method contains this line:

```
    g.drawImage( images[count++], 1, 1, this );
```

The last argument being passed to **drawImage** is a reference to **this** JApplet object. This call is actually to the ImageObserver interface, which comes from the Component class, of which JApplet is a direct descendant. The effect of ImageObserver is to automatically call **repaint( )**

if the picture is not available when requested. Because we are incrementing count in the same line, repaint will cycle through the whole catalogue. So we should remove the increment and the testing for the count equalling the number of frames and place them in the run section of the thread. That way ImageObserver will recall **paint( )** on the same picture, until it is complete. If we compile and run the program again, we see that it cycles through much as before, except that it loads the images one at a time, instead of every image every time. On the second pass, the animation begins to behave in a more sensible fashion. Is there a way we can cut out the first pass through the image list?

5.7.2 MediaTracker

We could load the images into a cache using a **MediaTracker** object to check that the image is fully loaded. This would delay the paint method until all the images are checked. First we declare an object cache of type **MediaTracker**. Next, when we are loading the pictures into the images array, we register them with the **MediaTracker** with this line:

```
cache.addImage(pictures[i], i);
```

The second argument to **cache.addImage** sets a flag that we can check later. It is convenient to use the picture number, so that we know which picture is causing the problem, if there is a problem at run time.

```
import javax.swing.*;
import java.io.*;
import java.awt.*;

public class Smile1 extends JApplet implements Runnable
{
    private Thread animate;
    private Image images[ ];
    private int frames = 20;
    private int count = 0;
    private MediaTracker cache;

    public void init( )
    {
        frames = 20;
```

```
      count = 0;
      images = new Image[frames];
      cache = new MediaTracker(this);
      for (int i = 0; i < frames; i++ )
      {
         images[i] = getImage(getDocumentBase( ), "Smile"
            + i + ".gif");
         cache.addImage(images[i], i);
      }
   }

   public void paint(Graphics g)
   {
      g.drawImage(images[count], 1, 1, this);
      if (count == frames) count = 0;
      System.out.println("Picture " + count + " painted");
   }

   public void start( )
   {
      if (animate == null)
      {
         animate = new Thread(this);
         animate.start( );
      }
   }

   public void run( )
   {
      for (int i=0; i < frames; i++)
      {
         System.out.println("Loading Image: Smile"+i );
         try
         {
            cache.waitForID(i);
         }
         catch (InterruptedException e)
           {
              System.out.println("Exception: "+ e.getMessage( ));
           }
         if (cache.isErrorID(i))
```

```
        {
            System.out.println("Error loading Smile"+ i );
            return;
        }
    } // end for
    while (isActive( ))
    {
        try
        {
            System.out.println("Calling paint....");
            repaint( );
            count++;
            if (count==frames)
            {
                count = 0;
            }
            Thread.sleep(1000);
        }
        catch (Exception e)
        {
            System.out.println("Exception: "+ e.getMessage( ));
        }
    } // end while
  } // end run( ) method
} // end class
```

The code in the **run( )** function does the same job as before, but before
it does that we want to force the program to check that all our pictures
have been loaded.

```
for (int i=0; i < frames; i++)
{
    // print whats happening to System window
     System.out.println("Loading Image: Smile"+ i );
    try
    {
        // check ID of each picture as loop increments
        cache.waitForID(i);
    }
    catch (InterruptedException e)
    {
```

```
      System.out("Exception: "+ e.getMessage( ));
   }
   if (cache.isErrorID(i))
   {
     // If any picture is not loaded then let us know
     System.out.println("Error loading Smile"+ i );
     return;
   }
}
```

This section of code cycles through the **MediaTracker** object cache and checks that the flag is set correctly. If a picture were unavailable for any reason, this section would throw an exception. The **try....catch** sequence allows us to put code in place to deal with a problem that may occur during file transfer – if we are dealing with an Internet download. This type of exception is possible, but unlikely, on a standalone PC. We can proceed by checking for a particular ID and printing a warning message if we find it. The empty braces immediately after the **catch (InterruptedException e)** would contain code for dealing with an **InterruptedException.**

Running this program, the improvement should be radical, although there is still a problem with the first picture, and a slight flicker when the image changes. For this we need a technique called *double buffering*.

There are three types of method used with **MediaTracker** objects: one to register the picture, four to load the picture and two to check that the picture is loaded. The first type of method, used to register the picture, can be in two forms.

AddImage(Image im, int x)	Registers the image *im* and associates it with a number.
AddImage(Image im, int x, int w, int h)	Registers an image to scale (width, height) and associates it with a number.

The picture can be loaded in four ways:

checkAll(true)	Starts loading and returns immediately.
checkID(int x, true)	Starts loading all images associated with integer *x* and returns immediately.

| **waitForAll( )** | Returns after the images are loaded. |
| **waitForID(int x)** | Loads images associated with integer *x* and returns when finished. |

The two methods used to check for errors in loading are:

| **isErrorAny( )** | Returns true if errors occurred. |
| **isErrorID(int x)** | Returns true if errors were encountered with images associated with integer *x*. |

In Swing, the **ImageIcon** class creates an Image and waits for it to load – unless you have a reason to use MediaTracker, it makes excellent sense to use ImageIcon to load and return the Image.

In the example try replacing the two lines

```
images[i] = getImage(getDocumentBase( ), "Smile" + i + ".gif");
cache.addImage(images[i], i);
```

with

```
images[i] = new ImageIcon("Smile" + i +".gif").getImage( );
```

not forgetting to remove all subsequent references to **cache**.

5.7.3 Double buffering

Double buffering is a technique used in AWT graphics to eliminate flicker in animations. In simple terms, we get the computer to render the graphics in an offscreen buffer, before transferring them to the screen. This means that the picture is transferred whole to the screen rather than built up on the screen. The program is developed from the previous program, these are the parts containing changed or extra code (in *italic*).

```
public class Smile extends Applet implements Runnable
{
    int count, frames;
    Image pictures[ ];
    Thread timer;
    Image offscreen;
    Graphics buffer;

    public void init( )
```

```
    {
        frames = 20;
        count = 0;
        pictures = new Image[frames];

        offscreen = this.createImage(100, 100);
        buffer = offscreen.getGraphics( );

        for (int i = 0; i < frames; i++ )
        {
            pictures[i] = new ImageIcon("Smile" + i + ".gif").getImage( );
        }
    }
```

We declare an object of type **Image**, which we call *offscreen*. This will
be used as a graphics context, matching the width and height of the
onscreen drawing area exactly. In order to draw it to the screen, we
need to pass it to a Graphics object which we will call *buffer*. We can
copy it to *buffer* using the **getGraphics( )** method.

```
    public void paint(Graphics g)
    {
        buffer.setColor(Color.white);
        buffer.fillRect(1, 1, 100, 100);
        buffer.drawImage(pictures[count], 1, 1, this);
        System.out.println("Printing smile" + count +" to the buffer");
        g.drawImage(offscreen, 1, 1, this);
        System.out.println("printing buffer to the screen");

        if (count == frames)
            count = 0;
    }
```

The **paint( )** method is now changed, and we have a four-step process.
First we set the colour of the buffer to white, and draw a rectangle, in
order to clear the contents. We then draw the picture to the buffer
instead of to the screen. Finally we move the contents of the buffer to
the screen. The System.out lines are there to help see what is going on,
when the program is ready to be unleashed on the Internet they can all
be removed. It may still be a good idea to print a message to the
browser's status bar, using **showStatus( )**, in order to reassure the user
that something is happening while the pictures are loading.

You are probably wondering why we bother to change the background of the buffer to white. Because **repaint( )** is called in the **run( )** section, surely the background will be erased anyway, by the implicit call to **update( )**. This is true, except that **update( )** will not clear the buffer's background, only the onscreen background. To prevent the same job being performed twice, we can override **update( )** by including a rewritten version in our code:

```
update(Graphics g)
{
    paint(g);
}
```

This has the effect of restricting **update( )** to calling **paint( )**. As we are explicitly clearing the old image from the buffer by drawing a white rectangle there, the effect is to reduce the work done by the processor.

Note that Swing components provide their own double buffering. See Chapter 10 for an animation example.

5.7.4 Clipping

Clipping is a technique that is used to simplify moving an image across a static background – if the background does not change during the course of an animation, there is little point in drawing it every time we move a foreground object. This technique specifies an area that needs to be redrawn, which logically will include the area just vacated and the new area moved to. This is computed by measuring a rectangle around the moving picture and redrawing the union of position A and position B.

Figure 5.7 Clipping areas

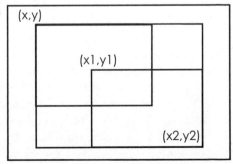

In Figure 5.7, the rectangle placed at (x, y) is moving to a new position at $(x1, y1)$. The union of both positions will be bounded by the area starting at (x, y) with an opposite corner at $(x2, y2)$.

The example below bounces a line of text up and down the screen. Where it passes across a colour, you will notice that the colour is replaced as the text passes across it. Where the text moves across an area without an image, there is nothing to redraw so the text remains. Notice in this applet that we use the **FontMetrics( )** method to find out how big the rectangle should be that includes all the text.

The line

```
Rectangle current = new Rectangle(x, y-sascent, swidth, sheight)
```

measures the current position of the string, using the variables sascent, swidth and sheight. We use sascent to ensure that we have no trail left by tall letters – remember that y increments downwards, so if we subtract the ascent from y we give ourselves headroom for the 't' and the 'h' in our string. We initialize these variables using **FontMetrics( )** like this:

```
FontMetrics fm = this.getFontMetrics(f);
swidth = fm.stringWidth(s);
sheight = fm.getHeight( );
sascent = fm.getAscent( );
```

Here is the complete code.

```
import javax.swing.*;
import java.awt.*;

public class BounceText extends JApplet implements Runnable
{
    private int Ylncr;

    private String s;
    private int swidth, sheight, sascent;

    private int x, y;
    private Color c1, c2, c3, c4, c5, c6;
    private Font f;
    private Thread animator;
```

```java
public void init( )
{
    s = "Watch this Groooovy movie";
    x = 10;
    y = 20;

    c1 = Color.red;
    c2 = Color.blue;
    c3 = Color.green;
    c4 = Color.yellow;

    f = new Font("TimesRoman", Font.BOLD, 30);

    FontMetrics fm = this.getFontMetrics(f);
    swidth = fm.stringWidth(s);
    sheight = fm.getHeight( );
    sascent = fm.getAscent( );
}

public void start( )
{
    animator = new Thread(this);
    animator.start( );
}

public void drawBack(Graphics g)
{
    g.setColor(c1);
    g.fillRect(0, 0, 300, 400);
    g.setColor(c2);
    g.fillRect(50, 50, 300, 400);
    g.setColor(c3);
    g.fill3DRect(100, 100, 300, 400, true);
}

public void paint(Graphics g)
{
    drawBack(g);
    g.setColor(c4);
    g.setFont(f);
    g.drawString(s, x, y);
}
```

```java
public void run( )
{
    while (true)
    {
        // get area of applet to use in movement algorithm
        Dimension d = this.getSize( );
        Rectangle current = new Rectangle(x, y - sascent,
            swidth, sheight);
        // test for top of bounce area
        if (y <= 20)
        {
            YIncr = 2;
        }
        if (y > d.height)
        {
            // when it gets to the bottom, send it up again!
            YIncr = -YIncr;
        }
        y = y + YIncr;

        // now calculate new rectangle
        Rectangle next = new Rectangle(x, y - sascent, swidth,
            sheight);
        // obtain union
        Rectangle r = next.union(current);
        Graphics2D g2 = (Graphics2D)getGraphics( );
        // repaint only the union area
        g2.clip(r);
        paint(g2);

        try
        {
            Thread.sleep(100);
        }
        catch(InterruptedException e)
            {
            System.out.println("Exception: " + e.getMessage( ));
            }
    } // end while
    } // end method
} // end class
```

Notice the line

```
g2.clip(r);
```

This is the line that restricts the redrawing to the rectangle r, which is produced from the union of the old rectangle and the new rectangle. Any call to **paint( )** coming after this line will be restricted to this rectangle.

5.8 Java2D features

Java2D is a major extension of the graphics capabilities of java.awt. It is implemented through the awt.Graphics2D class which extends awt.Graphics. Simplistically, this means that to use the features of Java2D we simply cast the appropriate graphics object to a Graphics2D object, and then use the Graphics2D classes wherever appropriate.

We will demonstrate this by showing how to use the **BasicStroke** object to set the width and style of a line, and the **GradientPaint** object to achieve a colour gradient.

Figure 5.8 Java2D GradientPaint and BasicStroke

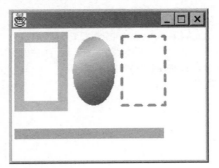

```
import javax.swing.*;
import java.awt.*;
import java.awt.geom.*;

public class TwoDDemo extends JFrame
{
    public TwoDDemo( )
    {
```

```
        setBackground(Color.white);
    }

    public void paint(Graphics g)
    {
        Graphics2D g2 = (Graphics2D) g; // cast g to Graphics2D

        g2.setPaint(Color.pink);
        g2.setStroke(new BasicStroke(15.0f));
        // define thickness of stroke
        g2.draw(new Rectangle2D.Double(15, 40, 65, 100));

        g2.setPaint(new GradientPaint(5, 30, Color.red, 35, 100,
            Color.yellow, true));
        g2.fill(new Ellipse2D.Double(95, 40, 65, 100));

        float[] sections ={10};
        g2.setPaint(Color.green);
        g2.setStroke(new BasicStroke(4, BasicStroke.CAP_ROUND,
            BasicStroke.JOIN_ROUND, 10, sections, 0));
        g2.draw(new Rectangle2D.Double(170, 40, 65, 100));

        g2.setPaint(Color.cyan);
        g2.setStroke(new BasicStroke(15.0f));
        g2.draw(new Line2D.Double(15, 180, 225, 180));
    }

    public static void main(String[] args)
    {
        JFrame f = new TwoDDemo();
        f.setSize(300, 300);
        f.show();
    }
}
```

The constructor for GradientPaint

```
g2.setPaint(new GradientPaint(5, 30, Color.red, 35, 100,
    Color.yellow, true));
```

Here the x, y coordinates 5, 30 specify the point we want the gradient to begin, and **Color.red** the starting colour. The coordinates 35, 100 specify the point the gradient ends and **Color.yellow**, the colour at the end of the gradient. The Boolean value *true* at the end specifies that if the end point is inside a larger area, then we want the gradient to repeat, back to the first colour.

The constructor for **BasicStroke**

```
g2.setStroke(new BasicStroke(4, BasicStroke.CAP_ROUND,
    BasicStroke.JOIN_ROUND, 10, sections, 0));
```

This is the fullest specification of five constructors for **BasicStroke**. Here, **4** represents the width of the line, **CAP_ROUND** specifies the rounded style of the end of the line, **JOIN_ROUND** specifies the style of a join between two lines, **10** specifies what is called the miterLimit – the overhead caused by two thick lines joining at an acute angle. This type of join may be squared off by specifying a smaller miterLimit. **Sections** is the name of an array of type **Float**. This array contains the intervals between dashes in a dotted or dashed line and the length of the dot or dash. By specifying ever greater numbers in this array it is possible to draw lines which begin as dots and end as dashes. Finally the **0** specifies the first cell in the array as a starting point for a phased progression (the array cycles back to the beginning when there are more dashes than cells).

SUMMARY

✓ This chapter has examined the Font class, drawing methods and taken a look at some simple animations. You should now know how to bring a graphic file to the screen, how to use graphics primitives to build up complex shapes and patterns.

✓ You should now also know how to animate pictures. We have looked at the techniques of animation, including the use of **mediaTracker** objects to monitor the loading of pictures, the use of threads to control the speed of an animation, the use of double buffering in conjunction with overriding the **update( )** method to smooth animation and the use of clipping to reduce the workload on the computer.

Exercises

❶ Create an animation using only double buffering and a thread.

❷ Create an animation that moves a small picture of a car across a background picture of a road.

❸ Draw a circle, using the rounded rectangle( ) method.

❹ Draw a grid for a game of noughts and crosses.

❺ Write a method that will draw an X or a O in a particular place on the screen. The method should take x, y coordinates as arguments.

❻ Modify the Bouncing Text applet so that the text moves in a diagonal and bounces off the sides as well as the top and bottom of the applet area.

6 | INTRODUCTION TO SWING

AIMS OF THIS CHAPTER

The aim of this chapter is to examine some of the components of the Java Swing package. We will be concentrating on the familiar components that make up a windows interface (buttons, checkboxes, comboboxes, etc.) and looking at the ways in which a Swing application differs from an AWT application. Visitors to the web site will be able to examine the code for AWT equivalents to many of the programs in this section.

6.1 About the AWT and Swing

The AWT contains classes that fall broadly into three categories. The first, *Graphics*, we have already looked at. The second category, *Components*, contains the GUI components commonly found in windowing systems – menus, buttons, etc. These components are added to a **Container** class such as **Frame** or **Panel** and arranged using classes from the third category, *Layout Managers*, of which we have already used **BorderLayout** and **FlowLayout**. To achieve an implementation that could be deployed on any platform, the language designers made use of 'peer classes', which handled the interaction between the local platform and its component. In other words, when we specify a button in our code, the host operating system supplies a button from its equivalent – Windows supplies a Microsoft-style button; X-Windows an X-Windows style button. The components available in the AWT were therefore restricted to a functional set of components that were readily available.

In **java.swing**, the designers have produced a much larger framework of components (many of which are described as lightweight, because they do not depend on peer classes) that are truly native to Java. Swing also allows the programmer some choice in the look and feel of the program.

6.2 A graphical user interface program

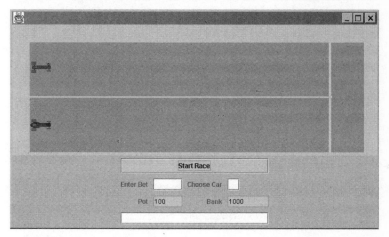

Figure 6.1 Drag racing GUI

The picture shows the latest stage in development of the drag racing game. The user interface that we described earlier has been implemented as a prototype application. The code for this is shown below. Don't panic – although it looks like heavy going, it is actually quite simple. We will look at everything that went into this program individually, and examine the implications of bundling it all together.

```
import javax.swing.*;
import java.awt.geom.*;
import java.awt.*;

public class RaceTrack extends JFrame
{
    private RaceTrackPanel animation;
    private JLabel betLabel, potLabel, bankLabel, carLabel;
```

```java
private JTextField betField, carField, potField, bankField,
   winnerField;
private JButton goButton;
private JPanel p;

public RaceTrack( )
{
   Image Track = new ImageIcon("Track.gif").getImage( );
   Image Car1 = new ImageIcon("Redcar.gif").getImage( );
   Image Car2 = new ImageIcon("Bluecar.gif").getImage( );
   animation = new RaceTrackPanel(this, Track, Car1, Car2);
   Container c = getContentPane();

   c.setLayout(new BorderLayout( ));
   p = new JPanel( );
   p.setBackground(Color.lightGray);
   GridBagLayout grid = new GridBagLayout();
   p.setLayout(grid);
   betLabel = new JLabel("Enter Bet");
   carLabel = new JLabel("Choose Car");
   potLabel = new JLabel("Pot");
   bankLabel = new JLabel("Bank");

   betField = new JTextField(5);
   carField = new JTextField(2);
   potField = new JTextField(5);
   bankField = new JTextField(7);
   winnerField = new JTextField(20);

   potField.setEditable(false);
   bankField.setEditable(false);

   goButton = new JButton("Start Race");
   GridBagConstraints gbc = new GridBagConstraints( );

   gbc.fill = GridBagConstraints.BOTH;
   gbc.insets = new Insets(5, 5, 5, 5);
   gblAdd(goButton, grid, gbc, 0, 0, 4, 1);

   gbc.fill = GridBagConstraints.NONE;
   gbc.anchor = GridBagConstraints.EAST;
   gblAdd(betLabel, grid, gbc, 0, 1, 1, 1);
```

```
      gbc.anchor = GridBagConstraints.WEST;
      gblAdd(betField, grid, gbc, 1, 1, 1, 1);

      gbc.anchor = GridBagConstraints.EAST;
      gblAdd(carLabel, grid, gbc, 2, 1, 1, 1);

      gbc.anchor = GridBagConstraints.WEST;
      gblAdd(carField, grid, gbc, 3, 1, 1, 1);

      gbc.anchor = GridBagConstraints.EAST;
      gblAdd(potLabel, grid, gbc, 0, 2, 1, 1);

      gbc.anchor = GridBagConstraints.WEST;
      gblAdd(potField, grid, gbc, 1, 2, 1, 1);

      gbc.anchor = GridBagConstraints.EAST;
      gblAdd(bankLabel, grid, gbc,2, 2, 1, 1);

      gbc.anchor = GridBagConstraints.WEST;
      gblAdd(bankField, grid, gbc, 3, 2, 1, 1);

      gbc.fill = GridBagConstraints.BOTH;
      gblAdd(winnerField, grid, gbc, 0, 3, 4, 1);

      betField.setText("");
      potField.setText("100");
      bankField.setText("1000");

      c.add("Center", animation);
      c.add("South", p);
   }

   private void gblAdd(Component c, GridBagLayout
      grid,GridBagConstraints gbc, int x, int y, int w, int h)
   {
      gbc.gridx = x;
      gbc.gridy = y;
      gbc.gridwidth = w;
      gbc.gridheight = h;
      grid.setConstraints( c, gbc);
      p.add(c);
   }
```

```java
   public static void main(String[] args)
   {
      JFrame f = new RaceTrack( );
      f.setSize(700, 400);
      f.show();
   }
}

class RaceTrackPanel extends JPanel
{
   RaceTrack holder;

   Image Track, Car1, Car2;
   int XPos, YPos;

   public RaceTrackPanel(RaceTrack app, Image Track,
      Image Car1, Image Car2)
   {
      this.Track = Track;
      this.Car1 = Car1;
      this.Car2 = Car2;
      setSize(600,270);
      setBackground(Color.darkGray);
      holder = app;

      XPos = 30;
      YPos = 30;
   }

   public void paintComponent(Graphics g)
   {
      super.paintComponent(g);
      int w;
      int h;
      w = Track.getWidth(this);
      h = Track.getHeight(this);
      if ((w>0) && (h>0))
      {
         g.drawImage(Track, XPos, YPos, this);
      }
```

```
      w = Car1.getWidth(this);
      h = Car2.getHeight(this);
      if ((w>0) && (h>0))
      {
         g.drawImage(Car1, XPos, YPos +25, this);
         g.drawImage(Car2, YPos, YPos +130, this);
      }
   }
} // end class
```

The first thing to notice is that we have defined a new class called
RaceTrackPanel, which extends **JPanel**. This class provides a 'canvas' for the graphics and will supply the animation when we implement the final stages of the application.

Why do we need a panel to hold the graphics?

6.3 Containers

Panels are created using the class **JPanel**, which is a sub-class of
JComponent, itself a sub-class of **Container**. We can say therefore
that **JPanels** are descended from the **Container** class, which means
that we can place components on a **JPanel**.

The programs below illustrate the use of a **JPanel** for containing GUI
components, graphics and both together.

6.3.1 JPanel

```
import javax.swing.*;
import java.awt.*;

public class MyPanel extends JFrame
{
   private JPanel p;
   private JLabel text;

   public MyPanel( )
   {
      Container c = getContentPane();
      // set colour of background
      c.setBackground(Color.black);
```

```
        // set Layout Manager
        c.setLayout(new BorderLayout());
        // instantiate Panel object
        p = new JPanel( );
        // set colour of Panel
        p.setBackground(Color.white);
        // instantiate a Label object to be contained by Panel
        text = new JLabel("This text is sitting in a white panel on a
            black background");
        // add Label object to Panel
        p.add(text);
        // add Panel to container
        c.add("South",p);
    }

    public static void main(String[] args)
    {
        JFrame f = new MyPanel();
        f.setSize(400, 100);
        f.show();
    }
}
```

Figure 6.2 Using a JPanel in an application

The application is derived from **JFrame**, itself derived (ultimately) from **Frame**. This means that we can use it to contain a component – **Jpanel** – upon which we can place a **JLabel** object. Note that the layout manager provided by the AWT for JFrame – **BorderLayout** – sets the position of the JPanels.

Examine the code in the constructor of the drag racing game at the beginning of the chapter. Try to work out the hierarchy of containers and see which Layout Manager is being used by which container.

6.4 Providing interactivity

The real power of GUIs lies in the fact that they offer the user an element of control. This is mainly achieved through choice and selection.

We have seen in the last few examples how Labels can be used to provide textual information. These may be instructions associated with another component or simply a label for a component. Labels we have used so far have all contained text of some kind, and we have seen the methods **setText( )** and **getText( )** demonstrated in Chapter 4. We will now take a look at some of the other familiar Windows elements such as **Buttons** – push buttons, checkboxes, choice buttons, how we can use checkboxes in groups to form radio buttons and finally scrollable lists.

First we will look at the simple push button.

6.4.1 Push button

```java
import java.awt.*;
import java.awt.event.*;
import javax.swing.*;
public class MyButton extends JFrame implements ActionListener
{
    private JButton b;
    private JTextField t;
    private int num, result;

    public MyButton( )
    {
        Container c = getContentPane();
        c.setLayout(new FlowLayout());
        b = new JButton("Double");
        b.addActionListener(this);
        t = new JTextField(7);
        t.setText("100");

        c.add(b);
        c.add(t);
    }
```

```java
    public void actionPerformed(ActionEvent e)
    {
        num = Integer.parseInt(t.getText());
        result = num * 2;
        t.setText( Integer.toString(result));
    }

    public static void main(String[] args)
    {
        JFrame f = new MyButton();
        f.setSize(300, 100);
        f.show( );
    }
}
```

This code provides a JTextField which holds a number. When the "Double" button is pressed, the number is multiplied by two and the new answer displayed. If a further button with a trebling effect is needed, **JButton b1**, then a condition would be required in the **actionPerformed( )** method:

```java
    if (e.getSource( )== b)
        result = num * 2;
    else
        result = num * 3;
```

You might try rewriting this program adding two more buttons, one to triple the figure and one to return the figure to 0.

6.4.2 Checkboxes

```java
import java.awt.*;
import java.awt.event.*;
import javax.swing.*;
public class MyCheckBox extends JFrame implements
    ItemListener
{
    private JCheckBox bold, italic;
    private JTextField t;
    private Font f;
    private int fontValue;
```

```
   public MyCheckBox( )
   {
      Container c=getContentPane();
      c.setLayout(new FlowLayout());
      f = new Font("TimesRoman", Font.PLAIN, 16);
      bold = new JCheckBox("Bold");
      bold.addItemListener(this);
      italic= new JCheckBox("Italic");
      italic.addItemListener(this);
      t = new JTextField(30);
      t.setFont(f);
      t.setText("We're off to see the Wizard!");
      c.add(t);
      c.add(Bold);
      c.add(Italic);
   }

   public void itemStateChanged(ItemEvent e)
   {
      if ((e.getSource()==italic)||(e.getSource() == bold))
      {
         fontValue=(bold.isSelected( ) ? Font.BOLD : 0) +
            (italic.isSelected( ) ? Font.ITALIC : 0);
      }
      t.setFont(new Font("TimesRoman", fontValue, 16));
      t.repaint( );
   }

   public static void main(String[] args)
   {
      JFrame f = new MyCheckBox();
      f.setSize(350, 100);
      f.show();
   }
}
```

Figure 6.3 A checkbox

The only bit of this code that requires explanation should be the **itemStateChanged** method. The same result could have been achieved with a series of IF statements, each one setting the font explicitly but this would have been repetitive and one thing programmers like to avoid is needless repetition. Here we take advantage of the fact that **Font.BOLD**, **Font.PLAIN** and **Font.ITALIC** are integer values. This means that we can test for the box being checked and represent the result as a number. For bold, the statement

```
FontValue = (bold.isSelected( ) ? Font.BOLD : 0)
```

means that if bold is selected, x is equal to 1 (**Font.BOLD**). If it is not selected then x is equal to 0 (**Font.PLAIN**). **Font.ITALIC** = 2 and the combination of both is equal to 3. This construction is very useful when checking a condition with only two outcomes.

The font style example is adequate for its purpose, but what if we wanted to change the font itself, or the size? Obviously we cannot have a font that is both Helvetica and Times New Roman in the way that we can have a font that is both bold and italic. There are two alternatives: either we write some extra code to set the other options to false or we look to the Java libraries again. We have two ready-made constructs for this eventuality. The first is known as a *combo box*.

6.4.3 Combo boxes

```
import java.awt.*;
import java.awt.event.*;
import javax.swing.*;

public class MyChoiceCheck extends JFrame implements
    ItemListener
{
    private JCheckBox bold, italic;
    private JComboBox fontName;
    private JTextField t;
    private Font f;
    private String[] items;
    private String fName;
    private int fontValue;

    public MyChoiceCheck( )
```

```java
    {
        Container c = getContentPane();
        c.setLayout(new FlowLayout());
        items = new String[]{"TimesRoman", "Helvetica", "Courier"};
        f = new Font("TimesRoman", Font.PLAIN, 16);
        bold = new JCheckBox("Bold");
        bold.addItemListener(this);
        italic = new JCheckBox("Italic");
        italic.addItemListener(this);
        fontName = new JComboBox(items);
        fontName.addItemListener(this);
        t = new JTextField(30);
        t.setFont(f);
        t.setText("We're off to see the Wizard!");

        c.add(t);
        c.add(bold);
        c.add(italic);
        c.add(fontName);
    }

    public void itemStateChanged(ItemEvent e)
    {
        if ((e.getSource()==italic) || (e.getSource() == bold))
        {
            fontValue = (bold.isSelected( ) ? Font.BOLD : 0) +
                (italic.isSelected( ) ? Font.ITALIC : 0);
        }
        if (e.getSource( ) == fontName)
        {
            fName = (String)fontName.getSelectedItem( );
        }
        t.setFont(new Font(fName, fontValue, 16));
        t.repaint();
    }

    public static void main(String[] args)
    {
        JFrame f = new MyChoiceCheck();
        f.setSize(350, 100);
        f.show();
    }
}
```

Figure 6.4 A Combo box

Adding the choice box is relatively straightforward: we declare a new
JComboBox object and put the names of the fonts into an array (items),
adding them explicitly to the object at instantiation, by-passing the
array as a parameter. When we get to the ItemStateChanged method,
we simply add another part to the if statement:

```
if (e.getSource( ) == fontName)
{
    fName = (String)fontName.getSelectedItem( );
}
t.setFont(new Font(fName, fontValue, 16));
```

Note that we have replaced a specific font title with the variable **fName**
in the font instantiation – this allows us to feed it the name selected
from the combo box.

6.4.4 Radio buttons

Radio buttons are used when there are a limited number of mutually
exclusive choices. For example, on a mail-order form, the credit card
is likely to be Visa, MasterCard or Access, but never more than one at
a time.

Figure 6.5 A radio button

```
import java.awt.*;
import java.awt.event.*;
import javax.swing.*;
```

```
public class MyRadio extends JFrame implements ItemListener
{
    private ButtonGroup radio;
    private JRadioButton Visa, Access, MasterCard;
    private JTextField t;
    private Font f;

    public MyRadio( )
    {
        Container c = getContentPane();
        c.setLayout(new FlowLayout());
        f = new Font("TimesRoman", Font.BOLD, 16);
        t = new JTextField(30);
        t.setFont(f);
        t.setText("Credit Card is....");

        c.add(t);
        c.add(Visa = new JRadioButton("Visa", false));
        c.add(Access = new JRadioButton("Access", false));
        c.add(MasterCard = new JRadioButton("MasterCard", false));

        Visa.addItemListener(this);
        Access.addItemListener(this);
        MasterCard.addItemListener(this);

        radio = new ButtonGroup( );
        radio.add(Visa);
        radio.add(Access);
        radio.add(MasterCard);
    }
    public void itemStateChanged(ItemEvent e)
    {
        if (Visa.isSelected( ) == true)
        {
            t.setText("Credit Card is: Visa");
        }
        if (Access.isSelected( ) == true)
        {
            t.setText("Credit Card is: Access");
        }
        if (MasterCard.isSelected( ) == true)
```

```
      {
          t.setText("Credit Card is: MasterCard");
      }
   }

   public static void main(String[] args)
   {
      JFrame f = new MyRadio();
      f.setSize(400, 100);
      f.show();
   }
}
```

The constructor for a radio button is

```
Visa = new JRadioButton("Visa", false);
```

where the Boolean *false* ensures that the button is not checked on instantiation.

A set of radio buttons is actually a group of individual radio buttons, linked by a **ButtonGroup** object with the lines:

```
radio = new ButtonGroup( );
radio.add(Visa);
radio.add(Access);
radio.add(MasterCard);
```

6.4.5 Lists

We are now going to have a look at lists, and the context we are going to look at them in is that of a 'shopping basket'-style application. This one will allow us to choose the ingredients for a breakfast from one list, and see them displayed in another.

Figure 6.6 A list

```
import java.awt.*;
import java.awt.event.*;
import javax.swing.*;

public class Breakfast extends JFrame implements
   ActionListener
{
   private JList ingredients, meal;
   private JButton move;
   private String[] food;

   public Breakfast( )
   {
      Container c = getContentPane();
      c.setLayout(new FlowLayout());
      food = new String[]{"Corn Flakes", "Shredded Wheat",
         "Eggs", "Beans", "Mushrooms", "Rashers", "Tea",
         "Coffee", "Toast", "Croissant"}; // one line of code
      ingredients = new JList(food);
      ingredients.setVisibleRowCount(5);
      ingredients.setSelectionMode(ListSelectionModel.
         MULTIPLE_INTERVAL_SELECTION);

      move = new JButton(">>>");
      move.addActionListener(this);

      meal = new JList();
      meal.setVisibleRowCount(5);

      c.add(new JScrollPane(ingredients));
      c.add(move);
      c.add(new JScrollPane(meal));
   }

   public void actionPerformed(ActionEvent e)
   {
      meal.setListData(ingredients.getSelectedValues());
   }

   public static void main(String[] args)
   {
```

```
        JFrame f = new Breakfast();
        f.setSize(500, 175);
        f.show();
    }
}
```

This example, like JComboBox, uses an array to contain the items on the list:

```
    ingredients = new List(4, false);
```

The lines

```
    ingredients.setVisibleRowCount(5);
    ingredients.setSelectionMode(ListSelectionModel.
        MULTIPLE_INTERVAL_SELECTION);
```

set the number of items visible and the ability to select multiple items by using the Ctrl and Shift keys on the keyboard.

The **actionPerformed( )** method simply retrieves the selected items from one list and places them in the second list.

SUMMARY

✓ This chapter has covered the components section of the Java abstract windowing toolkit, and the basic set of widgets available in both the AWT and Swing packages, including buttons, checkboxes, choice buttons, labels, and lists. Previous chapters looked at the text components JTextField and JTextArea.

✓ We began the chapter with a look at a user interface for a game that demonstrated the use of containers to hold graphics and widgets, controlled by two layout managers: one to control the positioning of the two major components (panel and canvas) and another (gridBagLayout) to control the layout of the buttons and text fields on the control panel. The next chapter will examine layout managers in detail.

Exercises

❶ Add a list containing font size to the example in 6.4.3, and make it change the size of the font in the message displayed. To maintain good practice, you should make the TimesRoman menu item call the serif font, Helvetica the sans serif and Courier the monospaced.

❷ In the breakfast example, work out a method of displaying the price of each item in the list. Have the computer display the total price of a breakfast.

❸ Create an interface with three buttons on three panels. The button on each panel should change the background colour of the panel.

❹ In the breakfast example, allow multiple selection and implement a method to add the items selected to the second list. (**Clue**: you need an array to hold the items.)

❺ Write a program that will work out the repayments on a mortgage over 10 years, 25 years and 35 years. The program should allow the user to input the total amount borrowed and the interest rate. The length of the loan should be made via a radio button or a choice box.

7 | LAYOUT MANAGERS

AIMS OF THIS CHAPTER

We have looked at the components and containers used to build GUIs, and we have seen an example of a GUI 'in action', using layout managers to control the position of the various elements on the screen. We will take a closer look at the layout managers provided by the Java AWT. These are shown in section 7.1.

We will also take a look at a new layout manager supplied by Swing, called the BoxLayout – this is similar to the GridLayout, except that it allows the use of fillers called Struts to create space within a box and a component called Glue, which keeps the layout stable (relative distance between components) when the window is resized.

7.1 Layout managers

FlowLayout   Applets and Panels default manager, arranges elements left to right and top to bottom where there is more than one row.

BorderLayout Frame and JFrame's default manager, arranges elements into five areas, north, south, east, west and center, where center expands to fill unallocated space.

GridLayout   Elements are arranged in equal rows and columns, the number of which are defined by the programmer.

CardLayout   Elements are arranged into a 'stack', where only the top card is visible. Usually used to stack containers so that a part of a screen can be changed.

GridBagLayout The 'Mother of all Layout Managers', this is the most flexible and inevitably the most complicated. It allows the programmer to define a grid based on the smallest component and to specify how many cells each component will fill in a horizontal and vertical direction. Attempting to use this manager without a sketch of the proposed interface will seriously damage your mental well-being!

7.2 FlowLayout

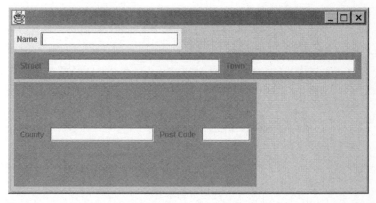

Figure 7.1 Three panels arranged with FlowLayout

The pictured application demonstrates the use of FlowLayout. Three panels, in different colours, have been placed upon the applet. The layout manager has been set to align all elements to the left in the code:

```
setLayout(new FlowLayout(FlowLayout.LEFT));
```

The word alignment property must be in capital letters. FlowLayout defaults to CENTER alignment.

The second panel illustrates that we can control the horizontal and vertical spacing of elements contained in the panel:

```
   p1.setLayout(new FlowLayout(FlowLayout.CENTER, 10, 10));
```

The last argument specifies the vertical spacing, the second argument the horizontal. The third panel illustrates the effect of increasing the vertical spacing.

```java
import java.awt.*;
import javax.swing.*;

public class MyFlow extends JFrame
{
   private JTextField name, street, town, county, postCode;
   private JLabel nameLabel, streetLabel, townLabel,
     countyLabel;
   private JLabel postCodeLabel;
   private JPanel p, p1, p2;

   public MyFlow( )
   {
      Container c = getContentPane();
      // set Layout alignment for the JFrame
      c.setLayout(new FlowLayout(FlowLayout.LEFT));

      // instantiate first panel and set background colour
      p = new JPanel( );
      p.setBackground(Color.yellow);

      // instantiate second panel, set colour and specify spacing
      p1 = new JPanel( );
      p1.setBackground(Color.pink);
      // A panel is a container so we can call setLayout directly
      p1.setLayout(new FlowLayout(FlowLayout.LEFT, 10, 10));

      p2 = new JPanel( );
      p2.setBackground(Color.green);
      p2.setLayout(new FlowLayout(FlowLayout.LEFT, 10, 70));

      // instantiate all elements
      name = new JTextField(20);
      name.setEditable(true);
      street = new JTextField(25);
      street.setEditable(true);
```

```
        town = new JTextField(15);
        town.setEditable(true);
        county = new JTextField(15);
        county.setEditable(true);
        postCode = new JTextField(7);
        postCode.setEditable(true);

        nameLabel = new JLabel("Name");
        streetLabel = new JLabel("Street");
        townLabel = new JLabel("Town");
        countyLabel = new JLabel("County");
        postCodeLabel = new JLabel("Post Code");

        // add elements to their panels
        p.add(nameLabel);
        p.add(name);

        p1.add(streetLabel);
        p1.add(street);
        p1.add(townLabel);
        p1.add(town);

        p2.add(countyLabel);
        p2.add(county);
        p2.add(postCodeLabel);
        p2.add(postCode);

        // add completed panels to container
        c.add(p);
        c.add(p1);
        c.add(p2);
    }

    public static void main(String[] args)
    {
        JFrame f = new MyFlow();
        f.setSize(200, 200);
        f.show();
    }
}
```

7.3 BorderLayout

BorderLayout is the default layout manager for Windows and the **Window** sub-class **JFrame**, which are mainly used in applications. Applets do not tend to use **Window** and **JFrame** because applets are embedded in the context of an HTML page, whereas applications require window management (a frame can be used with an applet to create a free floating 'window' associated with the applet). **BorderLayout** may still be used as a layout manager for Applets, where circumstances require it.

The example shows how a typical BorderLayout looks. There are up to five areas in a BorderLayout. When all five are used, the arrangement will look like the applet pictured in Figure 7.2; if the East or West area are missing, the Center area expands to take up the slack. If North or South are missing, the Center Area and East/West fill the remaining space.

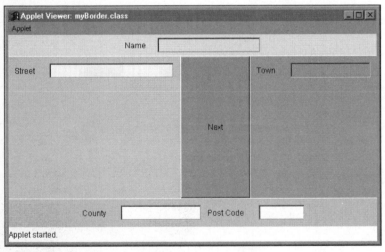

Figure 7.2 The BorderLayout

The code for this applet is not substantially different. The fields have been distributed among four panels and a button has been introduced for the centre position. The look of a BorderLayout depends on the dimensions of the applet area or the window containing it. The centre position is the last one to be calculated and its size depends on how much room is left after the other elements have been arranged.

```
setLayout(new BorderLayout(1, 1));
```

is used instead of

```
setLayout(new FlowLayout(FlowLayout.LEFT);
```

The arguments given to BorderLayout control the width and height of the border separating each component from the nest. In this case one pixel has been chosen.

The allocation of elements to areas is done when they are added to the container **c**.

```
c.add("North", p);
c.add("West", p1);
c.add("East", p2);
c.add("South", p3);
c.add("Center", b);
```

where **b** in the last line is a JButton.

Again, note that this may be used in conjunction with other layout managers and other components to produce sophisticated nested layouts.

7.4 GridLayout

GridLayout predictably arranges the components in a programmer-specified grid. Each component is the same size and we can specify horizontal and vertical spacing between components. This layout is ideal for creating displays of buttons or keypads, as seen in the calculator applet. Figure 7.3 shows a part of a computer keyboard.

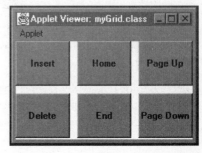

Figure 7.3
Buttons arranged with
GridLayout

```java
import javax.swing.*;
import java.awt.*;

public class MyGrid extends JFrame
{
    private JButton b1, b2, b3, b4, b5, b6;

    public MyGrid( )
    {
        Container c = getContentPane();
        // instantiate Buttons
        b1 = new JButton("Insert");
        b2 = new JButton("Home");
        b3 = new JButton("Page Up");
        b4 = new JButton("Delete");
        b5 = new JButton("End");
        b6 = new JButton("Page Down");

        /* Set layout to 2 rows and 3 columns, separated by 10
        pixels each way. */
        c.setLayout(new GridLayout( 2, 3, 10, 10));

        // add buttons to container
        c.add(b1);
        c.add(b2);
        c.add(b3);
        c.add(b4);
        c.add(b5);
        c.add(b6);
    }

    public static void main(String[] args)
    {
        JFrame f = new MyGrid();
        f.setSize(400,200);
        f.show();
    }
}
```

7.5 CardLayout

The CardLayout manager is used where it is convenient to let the user navigate through a series of screens from a list, or via push buttons. An example of such an application would be a personal information manager where the user selects Diary, Notepad or Address Book and the appropriate format is summoned to the screen (Figure 7.4).

It works by storing the components in a stack, like a pack of cards, so that only the top component is visible.

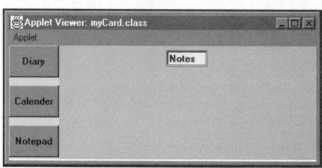

Figure 7.4 A personal information manager using CardLayout

In the pictured application, clicking on one of the buttons to the left will bring the appropriate card to the top of the pile. At the moment, Notepad is displayed.

```
import java.awt.*;
import java.awt.event.*;
import javax.swing.*;

public class MyCard extends JFrame implements ActionListener
{
    private JTextField dText, cText, nText;
    private JTextArea dEntry;
    private JButton diary, cal, note;
    private JPanel bpanel, cards, dpanel, cpanel, npanel;
    private CardLayout cl;

    public MyCard( )
    {
```

```java
Container c = getContentPane();
/*  use a border layout to position the control panel and
 * the 'pack' of cards   */

c.setLayout(new BorderLayout());

/* set up the control panel, we'll use a grid layout to hold
   the buttons */
diary = new JButton("Diary");
diary.addActionListener(this);
cal = new JButton("Calender");
cal.addActionListener(this);
note = new JButton("Notepad");
note.addActionListener(this);

bpanel = new JPanel( );
bpanel.setBackground(Color.yellow);
bpanel.setLayout( new GridLayout( 3, 1, 10, 10));
bpanel.add(diary);
bpanel.add(cal);
bpanel.add(note);

// now set up the components contained by each card.

// Diary Card
dpanel = new JPanel( );
dEntry = new JTextArea(5,20);
dText = new JTextField("April 1");
dpanel.add(dText);
dpanel.add(dEntry);

// Calendar Card
cpanel = new JPanel( );
cText = new JTextField("2000");
cpanel.setBackground(Color.green);
cpanel.add(cText);

// Notepad Card
npanel = new JPanel( );
nText = new JTextField("Notes");
npanel.setBackground(Color.pink);
npanel.add(nText);
```

```
      // Now create a container to hold the cards
      cards = new JPanel( );

      // instantiate a layout manager for it
      cl = new CardLayout( );
      cards.setLayout(cl);

      // now add the predefined cards
      cards.add("Diary", dpanel);
      cards.add("Calendar", cpanel);
      cards.add("Notes", npanel);

      /* finally, add the control panel and the pack of cards to
         the top level window */
      c.add("West", bpanel);
      c.add("Center", cards);
   }

   // show the card manager what to do when button is pressed!
   public void actionPerformed(ActionEvent e)
   {
      if (e.getSource() == diary)
      {
         cl.show(cards, "Diary");
      }
      else if (e.getSource() == cal)
      {
         cl.show(cards, "Calendar");
      }
      else if (e.getSource() == note)
      {
         cl.show(cards, "Notes");
      }
   }

   public static void main(String[] args)
   {
      JFrame f = new MyCard();
      f.setSize(200, 200);
      f.show();
   }
}
```

Probably the best way of coding a CardLayout is to code the hierarchy of components separately – deal with the top-level panels first and then add the individual cards, rather than attempting to code the whole thing in one go. The hierarchy of components in the example program is shown in Figure 7.5

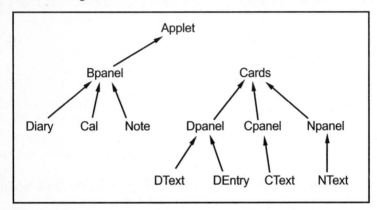

Figure 7.5 Component hierarchy for CardLayout

This application is only a skeleton; if it were to be developed properly, the hierarchy would extend several layers deeper, as components were added to give it the required functionality. It is therefore essential to work out what elements are included at which level before sitting down to code it. One useful strategy is to insert the panels you require before any other components. By setting the background colours temporarily, you can quickly see that your code is working properly, before you begin to add the detail.

The most noteworthy part of the code is the event handling. Because the layout manager is working in response to events, we must be able to pass messages back to it, and in this case the message is:

```
cl.show(Cards, "Calendar");
```

where the button clicked is **cal**. The layout manager has previously been assigned to a variable **cl**. Methods available to CardLayout include **show(Container, name)**, **next(Container)** and **previous(Container)**. The Container is the component that contains the panels; the name is only used with the **show( )** method, and is allocated to the component when it is added to its container. The components of a **CardLayout** are recorded by the layout manager in the order of addition.

```
cards.add("Calendar", cpanel);
```

where **cards** is the container panel, **cpanel** is the panel being added and **"Calendar"** is the name by which we will refer to it in the **show( )** method.

7.6 GridBagLayout

GridBagLayout is the most flexible of layout managers, but also the most complex. It builds on the GridLayout in that the layout is based on a grid, but differs in that components can fill more than one cell in the grid and therefore vary in size in the display. The way to devise a GridBagLayout is to draw the interface on paper first, and then make a grid that, if possible, encloses the smallest component. If that is not possible, then the grid should be based on either the width or the height of the smallest component.

In the grid in Figure 7.6, the Start Race button begins at column 0 and ends in column 3. Like arrays, the first element is 0, not 1.

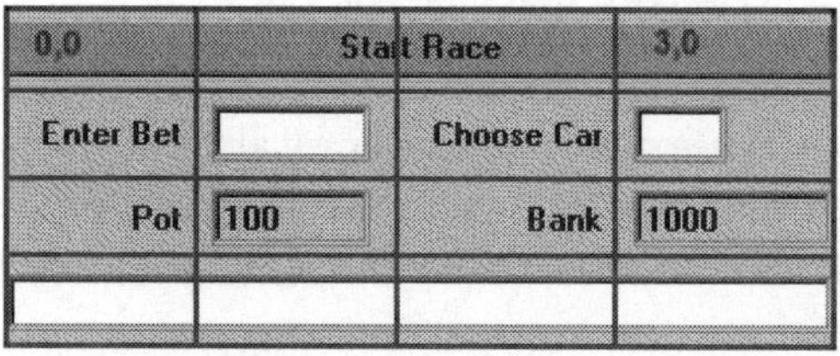

Figure 7.6 Design grid for GridBagLayout

Having decided on an appropriate grid we instantiate a **GridBagLayout** object. We do not tell it how many rows and columns it is dealing with yet; that is the job of a separate **GridBagConstraints** object.

```
GridBagLayout grid = new GridBagLayout( );
```

We now have a layout manager called **grid** and we assign it to the panel it will be managing – in this case, **p**:

```
p.setLayout(grid);
```

The next step is to construct a **GridBagConstraints** object. This will pass all the parameters for each cell in the grid to the **GridBagLayout** manager.

7.6.1   GridBagConstraints

The line

```
GridBagConstraints gbc = new GridBagConstraints( );
```

constructs the object. Now, for every element in the display we have to pass the following information:

gridx	Starting column
gridy	Starting row
gridwidth	Number of columns spanned
gridheight	Number of rows spanned
weightx	Amount of horizontal space allowed for expansion as a priority
weighty	Amount of vertical space allowed for expansion as a priority

In addition to this, we can also pass

ipadx	Internal horizontal padding
ipady	Internal vertical padding
insets	Margins to appear on all sides of component
anchor	Positions component in larger cell, using compass points and center as in GridLayout
fill	Specifies direction in which a component is allowed to grow if space is available. This could be NONE, BOTH, HORIZONTAL or VERTICAL.

Clearly there is much room for confusion here, as well as the potential for reams of repetitive code. The best way to approach it is to override the **add( )** function so that we can pass the component name, its position, breadth and depth at least as parameters. These are the vital parameters: everything else can be seen as 'fine tuning'. The idea is to get a layout that is close to ideal and then specify some of these other variables.

By doing this, we can convert

```
gbc.gridx = 0;
gbc.gridy = 0;
gbc.gridwidth = 4;
gbc.gridheight = 1;
Button goButton = new Button("Start");
grid.setConstraints( b, gbc);
p.add(goButton);
```

which we would have to repeat for every component, into

```
gblAdd(goButton, grid, gbc, 0, 0, 4, 1);
```

where we have defined a **gblAdd( )** function that looks like this:

```
private void gblAdd(Component c, GridBagLayout grid,
GridBagConstraints gbc, int x, int y, int w, int h)
{
    gbc.gridx = x;
    gbc.gridy = y;
    gbc.gridwidth = w;
    gbc.gridheight = h;
    grid.setConstraints(c, gbc);
    p.add(c);
}
```

This **gblAdd** function allows us quickly to add all the components in a style of code which we can easily follow.

```
gblAdd(goButton, grid, gbc, 0, 0, 4, 1);
gblAdd(betLabel, grid, gbc, 0, 1, 1, 1);
gblAdd(betField, grid, gbc, 1, 1, 1, 1);
gblAdd(carLabel, grid, gbc, 2, 1, 1, 1);
gblAdd(carField, grid, gbc, 3, 1, 1, 1);
gblAdd(potLabel, grid, gbc, 0, 2, 1, 1);
gblAdd(potField, grid, gbc, 1, 2, 1, 1);
gblAdd(bankLabel, grid, gbc,2, 2, 1, 1);
gblAdd(bankField, grid, gbc, 3, 2, 1, 1);
gblAdd(winnerField, grid, gbc, 0, 3, 4, 1);
```

Once this is in place, we should have a working program. To fine tune it, we can add the details immediately before the component we want to alter.

```
gbc.fill = GridBagConstraints.BOTH;
gbc.insets = new Insets(5, 5, 5, 5);
gblAdd(goButton, grid, gbc, 0, 0, 4, 1);
gblAdd(betLabel, grid, gbc, 0, 1, 1, 1);
```

etc. sets the fill and insets variables for all components until a newer instruction is placed.

```
gbc.fill = GridBagConstraints.BOTH;
gbc.insets = new Insets(5, 5, 5, 5);
gblAdd(goButton, grid, gbc, 0, 0, 4, 1);
gbc.insets = new Insets(10,10,10,10);
gblAdd(betLabel, grid, gbc, 0, 1, 1, 1);
```

The effect of the italicized line above is to alter the insets value from 5 all round to 10 all round.

Inserting this line before a **gblAdd( )** will display the following components to the left of the cell:

```
gbc.anchor = GridBagConstraints.WEST;
```

The example at the beginning of Chapter 6 contains the full code for the Drag Racing interface, using a variety of layout managers to place components correctly.

7.7 BoxLayout

BoxLayout is the default layout manager for the box class which is a type of container. The code below shows two ways of accomplishing the same button layout. The first method uses the container **Box**:

```
import java.awt.*;
import javax.swing.*;

public class MyBox extends JFrame
{
    private Box box;
    private JButton[] buttons;
    private String[] buttonLabels;

    public MyBox()
    {
        String[] buttonLabels ={"Menu", "Help", "Exit"};
```

```
      box = Box.createHorizontalBox();
      // box is a container!
      setContentPane(box);
      buttons = new JButton[3];
      for (int i = 0; i<=2; i++)
      {
         buttons[i] = new JButton(buttonLabels[i]);
         box.add(buttons[i]);
         box.add(Box.createHorizontalGlue());
      }
   }

   public static void main(String[] args)
   {
      JFrame f = new MyBoxLayout();
      f.setSize(200,70);
      f.show();
   }
}
```

The second method uses the layout manager to arrange the components on a container:

```
import java.awt.*;
import javax.swing.*;

public class MyBoxLayout extends JFrame
{
   private Box box;
   private JButton[] buttons;
   private String[] buttonLabels;

   public MyBoxLayout()
   {
      Container c = getContentPane( );
      // set the layout manager for c horizontally
      c.setLayout(new BoxLayout(c, BoxLayout.X_AXIS));
      String[] buttonLabels ={"Menu", "Help", "Exit"};
      buttons = new JButton[3];
      for (int i = 0; i<=2; i++)
      {
         //add glue before each button
```

```
        c.add(Box.createGlue( ));
        buttons[i] = new JButton(buttonLabels[i]);
        c.add(buttons[i]);
    }
}

public static void main(String[] args)
{
    JFrame f = new MyBoxLayout();
    f.setSize(200,70);
    f.show();
}
}
```

The BoxLayout uses two transparent filler components to create space between visible components – the one used here, **Glue,** adjusts space equally when the container is resized. Another, **Strut,** uses a fixed number of pixels to define a constant size.

```
Box.createVerticalStrut(10); // creates strut of height 10 pixels
Box.createHorizontalStrut(10); // creates strut of width 10 pixels
```

It is the use of these filler component that gives BoxLayout the flexibility missing from GridLayout and FlowLayout.

SUMMARY

✓ We have now dealt with the common layout managers in some detail. The essential lesson is always to opt for the simplest layout manager.

✓ The second most important thing is always to put some time into thinking about the design of your interface – you will quickly tie yourself in knots by attempting to code interfaces from scratch. If you are not using a visual IDE, then make a design first and then work out the most efficient way of implementing it.

Exercises

❶ Design an interface for an on-line art gallery. The user will need to see each picture and read some details about the artist.

❷ Design an interface for an on-line catalogue. Half the screen should contain the items for sale, the other half should contain fields allowing the user to fill in their name, address and credit card details and buttons to select different pages from the catalogue.

❸ Design an interface for a car dashboard. It should contain the speedometer and rev counter as large central objects, surrounded by fuel level, oil warning, brake light, head-light, indicator and temperature gauges.

❹ Design the layout for an e-mail application. There should be space for the user to write the message, and text fields for the user to fill in the e-mail address, the Description and the Copy to address. There should also be buttons to send the message and to clear the screen.

❺ Design an interface for a travel agent that allows the user to select items from a series of lists and buttons. The lists should be flight details, destination, length of stay, self-catering or half-board, and dates of stay.

8 | EVENT HANDLING AND GUI DESIGN

AIMS OF THIS CHAPTER

Central to the focus of this chapter is the event-handling model first released with JDK 1.1. In Java2, this event-handling model is integral to programming with GUIs in particular.

So far in this book we have used one method of event handling – by implementing a Listener interface we can have an object trap its own events and handle them using an actionPerformed method or equivalent. We will see that there are other architectures such as inner classes and anonymous inner classes that may be used, and one class can be used to handle all events in an application.

We will look at the some of the advanced widgets available in Java – including menus, scrollbars and dialogue boxes. We will also examine the use of inner classes to provide 'controller' logic and the advantages it brings.

8.1 Event handling

Different categories of objects trigger different types of event. This means the code that deals with an event is bound directly to the specific object. Let's take a look at a simple example of the model in action:

```
import java.awt.*;
import java.awt.event.*;
import javax.swing.*;
```

```
//We are going to implement the ActionListener interface
public class MyNewButton extends JFrame implements
   ActionListener
{
   private JButton b;
   private JTextField t;
   private int num, result;

   public MyNewButton( )
   {
      Container c = getContentPane();
      b = new JButton("Double");

      // now associate the ActionListener with the button
      b.addActionListener(this);

      t = new JTextField(7);
      t.setText("100");

      c.add("North",b);
      c.add("South",t);
   }

/* ActionListener has only one method – actionPerformed,
 * which we must implement */
   public void actionPerformed(ActionEvent e)
   {
      num = Integer.parseInt(t.getText());
      result = num * 2;
      t.setText(Integer.toString(result));
   }

   public static void main(String[] args)
   {
      JFrame f = new MyNewButton();
      f.setSize(100, 100);
      f.setVisible(true);
   }
}
```

In this example we are implementing the ActionListener interface, which has only one method – **actionPerformed(ActionEvent e)**. The event handler is the class, which has been notified that the event is fired by the button.

What happens if we have more than one button? Simple – any component that generates an **ActionEvent** (there are four: Button, List, MenuItem and TextField), can be assigned to an **ActionListener**. The **ActionEvent** can use the **getActionCommand( )** method to obtain the action command string. If no string has been explicitly set, then it simply returns the label of the component. Now that we can tell which component was responsible for the **ActionEvent**, we can write appropriate code to deal with it.

```java
import java.awt.*;
import java.awt.event.*;
import javax.swing.*;

public class MyNewTwoButtons extends JFrame implements
    ActionListener
{
    private JButton b, b1;
    private JTextField t;
    private int num, result;

    public MyNewTwoButtons()
    {
        Container c = getContentPane();
        b = new JButton("Double");
        b.addActionListener(this);
        // set tag for ActionListener to recognize button b by.
        b.setActionCommand("2");
        b1 = new JButton("Treble");
        // the code doesn't require a tag, but it works both ways!
        b1.addActionListener(this);
        t = new JTextField(7);
        t.setText("100");

        c.add("North",b);
        c.add("Center",t);
        c.add("South",b1);
    }
```

```
    public void actionPerformed( ActionEvent e)
    {
       num = Integer.parseInt(t.getText( ));
       String s = e.getActionCommand( );
       if (s == ("2"))
       {
          result = num * 2;
       }
       else if (s == ("Treble"))
       {
          result = num * 3;
       }
       t.setText( Integer.toString(result));
    }

    public static void main(String[] args)
    {
       JFrame f = new MyNewTwoButtons();
       f.setSize(200, 100);
       f.setVisible(true);
    }
  }
```

ActionListener is probably the most useful class provided in the new event model, and it is convenient to use it as it has only one method for us to implement. However, the AWT provides other classes with other interfaces, such as **WindowListener** and **MouseListener**, both of which will be useful but may have more methods than we actually need. We can skate around this problem by implementing the methods as skeletons containing no code, but this would require tedious and repetitive work and will make the program larger and harder to understand. Fortunately Java provides an adapter class for each interface that contains more than one method. This class implicitly implements empty versions of all the methods. To use an adapter class, we create a sub-class of it, thus inheriting all the methods. This, however, is very limiting, as Java does not allow multiple inheritance – nearly all of the examples in this book extend one class or another. This precludes use of this technique for all but a very few programs. A solution to this problem is to use a new Java feature – *inner classes*.

8.1.1 Inner classes

Inner classes give us a way of using the adapter class by nesting it inside the class we are writing, in the form of a *local class* or an *anonymous class*.

```java
import java.awt.*;
import java.awt.event.*;
import javax.swing.*;

public class MyLocalButton extends JFrame
{
   private ActionListener al;
   private JButton b;
   private JTextField t;
   private int num, result;

   public MyLocalButton( )
   {
      Container c = getContentPane();
      b = new JButton("Double");
      al = new MyButtonListener();
      b.addActionListener(al);
      t = new JTextField(7);
      t.setText("100");

      c.add("North",b);
      c.add("South",t);
   }

   public static void main(String[] args)
   {
      JFrame f = new MyLocalButton();
      f.setSize(100, 100);
      f.setVisible(true);
   }

   class MyButtonListener implements ActionListener
   {
      public void actionPerformed(ActionEvent e)
      {
         num = Integer.parseInt(t.getText());
```

```
            result = num * 2;
            t.setText( Integer.toString(result));
      }
   }
}
```

The *container* class declares an instance of the 'helper' class. Because it is contained in the **MyLocalButton** class, the local class **MyButtonListener** enjoys the same access to methods and variables as any of the outer classes methods. In this example the local class manipulates the private variables of the outer class directly.

Even more concise, and ideal for classes that do not contain large quantities of code, is the concept of *anonymous classes*. These are defined by an expression, which means that they can be included within an assignment or a call to a method.

```java
import java.awt.*;
import java.awt.event.*;
import javax.swing.*;

public class MyNewInnerButton extends JFrame
{
   private JButton b;
   private JTextField t;
   private int num, result;

   public MyNewInnerButton( )
   {
      Container c = getContentPane();
      b = new JButton("Double");

      /* declare and define anonymous inner class, notice the
       * opening bracket before new, is not closed until the end
       * of the class definition.  */

      b.addActionListener(new ActionListener( ){
         public void actionPerformed(ActionEvent e)
         {
            num = Integer.parseInt(t.getText( ));
            result = num * 2;
```

```
            t.setText( Integer.toString(result));
        }
    // close both sets of brackets here, class and method call
    });

    t = new JTextField(7);
    t.setText("100");

    c.add("North",b);
    c.add("South",t);
}

public static void main(String[] args)
{
    JFrame f = new MyNewInnerButton();
    f.setSize(100, 100);
    f.setVisible(true);
}
}
```

Having kept rigidly to a set style of indentation and bracketing, at first glance the anonymous class does little to enhance the readability of our code; however it has two major benefits – it is very concise and it allows us to bind the event handling of an object to the point of addition. This makes the logic of the program a great deal easier to follow. An effective strategy for dealing with anonymous classes is to have them call methods from the outer class. For example, this definition could have been written with a call to a method **calc(int x),** which would have contained the few lines of code required to perform the calculation on integer x.

Compile these programs and take a look at the directory listing. You will see that the compiler has produced a class for each inner class, in addition to the outer class.

8.2 Frames

A Frame in Java Swing is encapsulated by the **JFrame** class – a subclass of **Window** – and is used either as a basis for a windows-style application or to provide an applet with a free-floating extra window.

First we will return to basics for a look at a simple application. The important thing about frame-based applications is that we have to provide a means of closing them. This is provided by the use of a **WindowListener** interface (note that this has not been provided in earlier examples).

```java
import java.awt.*;
import java.awt.event.*;
import javax.swing.*;

class MyFrame extends JFrame
{
    public MyFrame()
    {
        this.setBackground(Color.yellow);

        // anonymous inner class – note syntax carefully!
        addWindowListener(new WindowAdapter( ){
            public void windowClosing(WindowEvent e)
            {
                System.exit(0);
            }
        });
    }

    public void paint(Graphics g)
    {
        g.drawString("This is a simple frame", 35, 90);
    }

    public static void main(String[] args)
    {
        JFrame f = new MyFrame( );
        f.setSize(200, 200);
        f.show( );
    }
}
```

The example above is interesting in that it uses a different method of handling events than we have used up to now. Before this chapter we implemented **ActionListener** and provided an **actionPerformed( )**

method after registering the **ActionListener**. This was convenient because the syntax is clean and the **ActionListener** interface requires us to implement only a single method – **actionPerformed( )**. Unfortunately, WindowListener requires us to implement several other methods, such as **windowIconified( )** and **windowOpened( )**, none of which we are interested in here.

The solution is to use an anonymous inner class to handle the single event of closing the window from the icon in the top right-hand corner. We use an anonymous inner class because there is no data involved and the behaviour is so trivial it does not justify writing a class to encapsulate it. If you look in the directory after compiling the program, you will see an additional class signified by the $ sign – **MyFrame$1.class**.

The next example uses the same frame, this time invoked from an applet. There are some important differences in the class **MyFrame**. Firstly the main method has gone, the object being instantiated by the call from the applet. The rest of the functionality is provided by the constructor method, which is called in the applet's **actionPerformed( )** method when the frame is called. Secondly, in the frame's **windowClosing( )** method, we have replaced

```
System.exit(0);
```

with

```
dispose( );
```

The reason for this is that we want to close only the window, not the entire applet. The call to System would dispose of all resources associated with the window, including the program that called it. We would prefer the applet to continue running until we have finished using it!

```
import java.awt.*;
import java.awt.event.*;
import javax.swing.*;

public class MyAppletFrame extends JApplet implements
    ActionListener
{
    private MyFrame f;
```

```java
   private JButton b;

   public void init( )
   {
      Container c = getContentPane();
      b = new JButton("Click me - I'm a Button!");
      b.addActionListener(this);
      c.add(b);
   }

   public void actionPerformed(ActionEvent e)
   {
      if ( e.getSource( ) == b)
      {
         f = new MyFrame( );
      }
   }
}

class MyFrame extends JFrame
{
   public MyFrame( )
   {
      setBackground(Color.yellow);
      addWindowListener(new WindowAdapter(){
         public void windowClosing(WindowEvent e)
         {
            dispose( );
         }
      });
      setSize(200, 200);
      show( );
   }

   public void paint(Graphics g)
   {
      g.drawString("This is a simple frame", 35, 90);
   }
}
```

8.3 Menus

A menu is itself made up of components – at the top level **JComponent** is extended to provide **JMenuBar**. AbstractButton is extended to provide **JMenuItem**. **JMenuItem** is extended to provide **JMenu** and **JCheckboxMenuItem** (menu items that toggle between two states).

In Figure 8.1 we have a **JMenuBar** which supports three menus: Breakfast, Lunch and Action. The Breakfast menu has been accessed, showing a number of **JMenuItems** and three **JCheckBoxMenu** items.

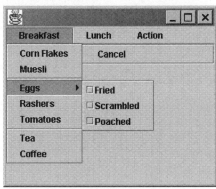

Figure 8.1 A menu

The coding is very simple: declare the **JMenuBar**, then one at a time add the **JMenus** and their **JMenuItems**. It is not syntactically necessary to code in this order, but by nesting the sub-menus you can see at a glance that all the intended items are in the correct menus. When the **JMenuItems** have been added, the **JMenu** is added to the **JMenuBar**. The final task is to write event handling code for all choices.

Here is the complete code.

```java
import java.awt.*;
import java.awt.event.*;
import javax.swing.*;

public class MyMenu extends JFrame implements ActionListener
{
    private double price = 0.00;
    private JButton b;
    private JMenuBar mb;
```

```java
private JMenu brek, e, l, a;
private JMenuItem corn, mues, rash, tom, tea, coff, steak,
   pasta, bill;

public MyMenu( )
{
   Container c = getContentPane();
   // instantiate MenuBar object
   mb = new JMenuBar( );

   // Declare Menu object
   brek = new JMenu("Breakfast");

   // Add items to Menu object
   corn = new JMenuItem("Corn Flakes");
   brek.add(corn);
   mues = new JMenuItem("Muesli");
   brek.add(mues);
   brek.addSeparator( );

   // This will be a submenu
   e = new JMenu("Eggs");
   e.add(new JCheckBoxMenuItem("Fried"));
   e.add(new JCheckBoxMenuItem("Scrambled"));
   e.add(new JCheckBoxMenuItem("Poached"));

   // Add submenu defined above, to Menu object
   brek.add(e);

   // note syntax to add action listener at instantiation
   (rash = new JMenuItem("Rashers")).addActionListener(this);
   brek.add(rash);
   brek.add(new JMenuItem("Tomatoes"));
   brek.addSeparator();
   brek.add(new JMenuItem("Tea"));
   brek.add(new JMenuItem("Coffee"));

   // add Breakfast Menu to Menu Bar
   mb.add(brek);

   // Create and add Lunch menu
   JMenu l = new JMenu("Lunch");
```

```java
        l.add(new JMenuItem("Steak"));
        l.add(new JMenuItem("Pasta"));
        mb.add(l);

        // Create and add Action Menu
        JMenu a = new JMenu("Action");
        // adding action listener at instantiation
        (bill = new JMenuItem("Bill")).addActionListener(this);
        a.add(bill);
        mb.add(a);

        // use Frame method to construct object
        setJMenuBar(mb);

        b = new JButton("Cancel");
        b.addActionListener(this);
        c.add("North", b);
    }

    /* As an example, we'll attach a price to one item only, and
    use the actionPerformed method as a quick Bill calculator */
    public void actionPerformed(ActionEvent e)
    {
        if( e.getSource() == b)
        {
            price = 0.0;
            System.out.println("Your tray is empty - You may start
                choosing again");
        }
        else if ((JMenuItem)e.getSource() == rash)
        {
            // price = price + 2.25
            price += 2.25;
        }
        else if ((JMenuItem)e.getSource() == bill)
        {
            System.out.println("Price is: " + price);
        }
    }

    public static void main(String[] args)
    {
```

```
        JFrame f = new MyMenu( );
        f.setSize(200, 200 );
        f.show( );
    }
}
```

In this example, we have implemented actions for only a couple of items on the menu. To implement the rest of the menu, **ActionListeners** must be added to all choices and **actionPerformed** altered to include the appropriate response to individual items.

8.4 Slider controls

To illustrate the use of a slider control, we could rewrite the temperature conversion program we looked at in Chapter 4 so that the centigrade value is input via a scrollbar (Figure 8.2).

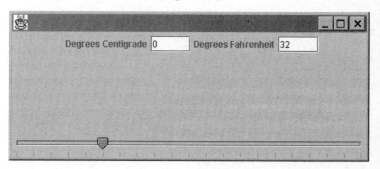

Figure 8.2 Temperature converter with slider control

The changes to the actual temperature converter are quite straightforward. A **JSlider** is declared, and instantiated with the lines:

```
Temp = new JSlider(SwingConstants.HORIZONTAL,-50, 150, 0);
Temp.setMajorTickSpacing(10);
Temp.setPaintTicks(true);
```

The arguments specify that this scrollbar is horizontal, the minimum value represented should be –50 and the maximum 150. The slider's starting value is 0. **setMajorTickSpacing(10)** sets ticks at intervals of 10 along the length of the slider and **setPaintTicks(true)** renders them visible.

The remaining components are deployed on their own panel, which takes up the rest of the area. **JSlider** events are handled by the **ChangeListener** interface and its **stateChanged()** method. Simply use **stateChanged()** to trap the value of the scrollbar, and pass it to **convert(int x)** which processes the placing of new text into the **TextFields**.

Note that this is again implemented by use of an anonymous inner class and that this class has access to the parent class's methods.

```java
import java.awt.*;
import javax.swing.*;
import javax.swing.event.*;

public class MySlider extends JFrame
{
    JPanel p;
    JSlider Temp;
    JLabel CentLabel, FarLabel;
    JTextField Centin, Farout;
    int f, c, answer;

    public MySlider( )
    {
        Container c = getContentPane();
        Temp = new JSlider(SwingConstants.HORIZONTAL,-50, 150, 0);
        Temp.setMajorTickSpacing(10);
        Temp.setPaintTicks(true);
        Temp.addChangeListener(new ChangeListener(){
            public void stateChanged( ChangeEvent e)
            {
                int Scroll;
                Scroll = Temp.getValue( );
                convert(Scroll);
            }
        });

        CentLabel = new JLabel("Degrees Centigrade");
        FarLabel = new JLabel("Degrees Fahrenheit");
        Centin = new JTextField (5);
        Farout = new JTextField(5);
        c.setBackground(Color.lightGray);
```

```
        p = new JPanel( );
        p.add(CentLabel);
        p.add(Centin);
        p.add(FarLabel);
        p.add(Farout);

        c.add("Center", p);
        c.add("South", Temp);

        // set initial values in textFields
        Centin.setText("0");
        Farout.setText("32");
    }

    public int calc(int x)
    {
        answer=(((9 * x)/5) + 32 );
        return answer;
    }

    public void convert(int x)
    {
        Centin.setText(Integer.toString(x));
        f = calc(x );
        Farout.setText(Integer.toString(f));
    }

    public static void main(String[] args)
    {
        JFrame f = new MySlider();
        f.setSize(500, 200);
        f.setVisible(true);
    }
}
```

8.5 Dialogue boxes

Dialogue boxes are pop-up boxes that are used in one of two modes, both of which will be familiar to Windows users. The first mode is known as *modal* – this is the box that will not allow the user to do anything until they have dealt with the dialogue box. An example of this is the warning box that appears if you try to save a file whose name is being used already. The second type is known as *modeless*, and this is the one that can be found in the *About* menu of most programs.

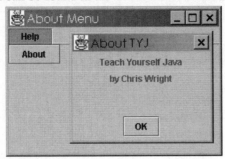

Figure 8.3 A dialogue box

This code produces the modeless box shown in Figure 8.3.

```java
import java.awt.*;
import java.awt.event.*;
import javax.swing.*;

public class MyDialog extends JFrame implements
   ActionListener
{
   private JMenuBar mb;
   private JMenu h;
   private JMenuItem about;

   public MyDialog( )
   {
      // captions the application
      super("About Menu");

      // create menubar to hold menu
      mb = new JMenuBar( );
      // create HelpMenu
      h = new JMenu("Help");
      (about = new JMenuItem("About")).addActionListener(this);
      h.add(about);

      mb.add(h);
```

```java
      // add Help menu to menubar
      mb.add(h);
      setJMenuBar(mb);
      setBackground(Color.lightGray);
   }

   public void actionPerformed(ActionEvent e)
   {
      if( e.getSource() == about)
      {
         // pass the box a reference to this object
         AboutBox a = new AboutBox(this);
         a.setSize(200, 150);
         a.setVisible(true);
      }
   }

   public static void main(String[] args)
   {
      JFrame f = new MyDialog( );
      f.setSize(200,200);
      f.setVisible(true);
   }
}

// define new class for Dialogue box
class AboutBox extends Dialog implements ActionListener
{
   JLabel l, l1;
   JButton b;
   JPanel p, p1;
   MyDialog parent;

/* constructor of the dialogue box, receives object of type
   Frame, i.e. MyDialog */

   public AboutBox(JFrame parent)
   {
      // false sets mode to modeless
      super(parent, "About TYJ", false);

      p = new JPanel( );
```

```
        l = new JLabel("Teach Yourself Java");
        l1 = new JLabel("by Chris Wright");
        p.add(l);
        p.add(l1);

        b = new JButton("OK");
        b.addActionListener(this);
        p1 = new JPanel( );
        p1.add(b);

        add("Center", p);
        add("South", p1);
        pack( );
        show( );
    }

    public void actionPerformed(ActionEvent e)
    {
        dispose( );
    }
}
```

8.6 Mouse events

Mouse events are provided with two adapter classes, **MouseAdapter**
and **MouseMotionAdapter**. The Listener methods provided by the
MouseAdapter class are:

mouseClicked( ) Where the user has pressed and released the button on a component without moving it

mouseEntered( ) Where the mouse pointer crosses the border of a
component

mouseExited( ) Where the mouse pointer leaves a component,

mousePressed( ) Where the mouse is 'clicked and dragged'

mouseReleased( ) Where the pressed button is released.

The **MouseMotionAdapter** class provides us with **mouseDragged( )**
which deals with events caused by 'clicking and dragging' and
mouseMoved( ), which deals with events caused by moving the mouse
without clicking.

In this program, which draws a line on the applet panel whilst echoing the mouse coordinates to the staus bar, we will use **mousePressed( )** to let us know where to start drawing, and **mouseDragged( )** to record the successive *x,y* coordinates. Note that we require our graphics context to be the applet, not the inner class.

The line

```
Graphics g = myNewCoordinates.this.getGraphics( );
```

uses the same technique as the dialog box program to ensure that the graphics context is the applet.

Here is the complete code for the program:

```
import java.awt.*;
import java.awt.event.*;
import javax.swing.*;

public class MyNewCoordinates extends JApplet
{
    private int lastX, lastY;
    private Color myColor = Color.blue;

    public void init()
    {
        this.setBackground(Color.red);
        this.addMouseListener(new MouseAdapter( ){
            public void mousePressed(MouseEvent e)
            {
                lastX = e.getX( );
                lastY = e.getY( );
            }
        });

        this.addMouseMotionListener(new MouseMotionAdapter( ){
            public void mouseDragged(MouseEvent e)
            {
                Graphics g = MyNewCoordinates.this.getGraphics( );
                g.setColor(myColor);
                int x = e.getX( );
                int y = e.getY( );
                g.drawLine( lastX, lastY, x, y );
```

```
            lastX = x;
            lastY = y;
            showStatus("Mouse is at: ("+ lastX + "," + lastY+")");
        } // end mouseDragged
    }); // end inner class
  } // end init
} // end class definition
```

SUMMARY

✓ This chapter is by no means a complete guide to the event model; rather it is intended to demonstrate ways in which we can use the event model in our programs. For complete documentation refer to the online resources listed at the end of this book.

✓ The use of inner classes enables us to bundle 'helper' classes with the class that they help, without going through the tortuous process of explicitly telling each class which other classes it knows about. This certainly makes working with classes a more intuitive process and should therefore enable us to increase our productivity. From the beginner's point of view, however, it does increase the complexity of the object model, especially as it effectively gives us a hierarchy of containment as well as one of inheritance.

✓ While every programmer establishes a method of working that is informed by their understanding of the language and by the types of application they are used to creating, I would suggest that a good way to approach inner classes is to use them only where the class is specifically designed to be bundled with one – and only one – application. If the class can be abstracted into a state where it might be reused in another application, such as the keyboard class in our calculator application, then it should be left as a standalone class. Using inner classes to deal with the event handling of an application is a good example of this kind of application-specific behaviour.

Exercises

❶ Rewrite the calculator program so that it becomes a free-floating window that can be summoned by clicking a button in an applet.

❷ Write an application that allows the user to write in a textArea. Menus should be available to allow the user to change font, style and size.

❸ Rewrite the temperature conversion program so that it is available as a pop-up window from an applet button.

❹ Write an application using JDK 1.1 event handling that allows the user to draw a picture on a JPanel. There should be a menu system allowing the user to select different colours for the drawing.

9 | INPUT/OUTPUT AND COMMUNICATIONS

AIMS OF THIS CHAPTER

The aim of this chapter is to examine very briefly how Java handles input and output at a local level in order to familiarize ourselves with basic principles, and then to look in greater depth at Internet level communica-tions. We will look at file handling (restricted in Java to applications), and at the way Java uses Stream, Reader and Writer classes for data transfer. At Internet level we will look at the concept of protocols, examining **http**, and **tcp**. We shall examine the classes provided by java.net and create a simple client and server as a demonstration of these classes. Finally we shall create an http-based browser that downloads and displays raw HTML from the Internet.

9.1 Introduction to I/O and networking

Input/Output (or I/O as it is usually referred to) refers to the methods a computer uses to read data in (input) from an external source such as a keyboard or a file, and to write data out (output) to an external source such as a monitor or a File. This model can be logically extended to include other computers and other networks. The Internet is an example of computers reading and writing to other computers on other networks.

Data is transmitted at a physical level as a stream of binary numerals, usually represented electronically by a square wave, where the peak represents a 1 and the trough a 0. Meaningful data can therefore be transmitted by a series of voltage fluctuations. The wire carrying the stream neither knows nor cares about the meaning of the 1s and 0s – what is important is that the sending device and the reading device both agree about the format of the data. In other words if our basic unit of information is to be a byte (series of eight 1s and 0s), then the receiver must know that the stream of binary data should be divided into byte-sized chunks for easier digestion. Java provides us with an attractively intuitive method of handling data transfer, with its use of byte stream classes, the most important of which are:

InputStream	**OutputStream**
BufferedInputStream	BufferedOutputStream
DataInputStream	DataOutputStream
FileInputStream	FileOutputStream
StringBufferInputStream	PrintStream

The disadvantage inherent in the use of byte-based classes for data transfer is that it does not handle text particularly efficiently, especially text containing symbols from an extended character set such as Cyrillic or Japanese, which requires more than one byte for certain characters.

Java also provides an analogous set of character-based input and output streams to deal with textual I/O, which are extended from Reader and Writer respectively. These are more efficient than byte streams and, because they convert characters into Unicode (using two bytes) for internal handling, are ideal for internationalized programs, where character sets may prove problematic for byte stream implementations.

BufferedReader	BufferedWriter
LineNumberReader	StringWriter
CharArrayReader	CharArrayWriter
FilterReader	FilterWriter
PushBackReader	
InputStreamReader	OutputStreamWriter
FileReader	FileWriter
PipedReader	PrintWriter
StringReader	StringWriter

Although it is not necessary at this stage to know all the details of every class provided for I/O in Java, we will look at some of the classes that are likely to be useful in our programs.

9.2 InputStream and OutputStream

These are abstract classes used as the base for the other stream classes. They provide an interface for reading and writing *bytes* of information.

9.2.1 How do they work?

All the programs we have written so far send a message to an object explicitly, by means of a function call. We obviously don't want to embed every part of every message we send along a cable inside that type of computer program – that would be wasteful. The solution to this quandary is that when we create an object of type **InputStream** we place it in an endless loop, which terminates only when data becomes available. This has the effect of the **InputStream** listening and waiting for action on the line, which is known as *blocking*. When a signal is received, the contents of the loop are invoked.

The most basic example of input and output in action is to read characters from the keyboard and write them to the screen. We therefore need to create a situation where the program listens for activity from the keyboard. This activity would be called *System input*.

The technique we use to create this listening loop requires *exception* handling, because we need to be able to escape from the loop if something goes wrong. An exception is *thrown* when a problem strikes. It is the programmer's job to *catch* these exceptions before they unexpectedly terminate the program. We can do this by creating a **try...catch** loop:

```
try
{
    // Some I/O activity or other
}
catch(Exception e)
{
    // What we do when exception e occurs
}
```

There are a number of known exceptions provided for in the language. These include **IOException**, which would be the one *thrown* here. All the known exceptions are sub-classes of **java.lang.throwable**.

We have used output from the system frequently in example programs as a means of providing feedback to the screen, so it should come as no surprise that the standard input and output variables provided by the **System** class are *in* and *out*.

9.2.2 StringBuffer

The StringBuffer object allows us to add characters into an expandable buffer. The contents can be printed out again with a call to the System output stream **out**.

```
import java.io.*;

class Keyboard
{
   public static void main(String[] args)
   {
      StringBuffer sb = new StringBuffer( );
      char c;

      try
      {
         // cast integer representation to char
         while ((c = (char)System.in.read( )) != '\n')
         {
            // add char to end of StringBuffer contents
            sb.append(c);
         }
      }
      catch(Exception e)
      {
         System.out.println("Exception: " + e.getMessage( ) +
         "has occurred");
      }

      System.out.println(sb);
   }
}
```

Once more the Java libraries make life simple. Here we are using the **StringBuffer** class to hold a variably sized string of characters, read in from the keyboard using the **InputStream** object **in**, terminated by the new line character (carriage return). The system reads the characters in from the keyboard and, when the user presses enter, prints the contents of the **StringBuffer** to the screen, using the OutputStream object **out**. We need to catch the possibility of an I/O exception, so we place the reading in of characters within a **try...catch** loop. The actual exception would be relayed to the screen by the **Throwable** method **getMessage( )**.

9.2.3 FileOutputStream

If we wanted to write the stream in the previous program to a file, we would use **FileOutputStream(filename)**:

```
import java.io.*;
class MyFile
{
   public static void main(String[] args)
   {
      StringBuffer sb = new StringBuffer();
      char c;

      try
      {
         while ((c = (char)System.in.read( )) != '\n')
         {
            sb.append(c);
         }
      }
      catch(Exception e)
      {
         System.out.println("Exception: " + e.getMessage( ) +
         "has occurred");
      }

      /* Now convert StringBuffer to a String and store in a
         byte Array,ready to pass to FileOutputStream. */
      String s = sb.toString( );
      byte[ ] buffer = s.getBytes( );
```

```
    // create a file myFile.txt and write contents of buffer to it.
    try
    {
      FileOutputStream out=new FileOutputStream("myFile.txt");
      out.write(buffer);
    }
    catch(Exception e)
    {
      System.out.println("Exception: " + e.getMessage( ) +
        "has occurred");
    }
  }
}
```

9.2.4 FileInputStream

To read from a file, we reverse the process:

```
import java.io.*;
class MyFile2
{
  public static void main(String[] args)
  {
    File f = new File("myFile.txt");
    int i = (int)f.length( );
    byte[ ] buffer = new byte[i];
    try
    {
      FileInputStream in = new
        FileInputStream("myFile.txt");
      in.read(buffer, 0, i);
    }
    catch(Exception e)
    {
      System.out.println("Exception: " + e.getMessage( ) +
        "has occurred");
    }
    String s = new String(buffer);
    System.out.println(s);
  }
}
```

In this example, we check to find out how long the file is, create a byte array of that length to hold it and read it into the array using a **FileInputStream** object.

9.2.5 InputStreamReader and PrintWriter

The **InputStreamReader** class takes an input stream as a parameter and may be passed to a BufferedReader, which allows us to extract the contents as a String.

```java
import java.io.*;

class Dinput
{
    public static void main(String[] args)
    {
    /* Step 1 - InputStreamReader read = new
                    InputStreamReader(System.in);
        Step 2 - BufferedReader bread = new
                    BufferedReader(read);
        Step 3 - can be shortened to:   */

        BufferedReader bread = new BufferedReader(new
            InputStreamReader(System.in));
        String s = new String( );

        try
        {
            s = bread.readLine( );
        }
        catch(Exception e)
        {
            System.out.println("Exception: " + e.getMessage( ) +
            "has occurred");
        }
        System.out.println(s);
    }
}
```

PrintWriter takes an output stream as a parameter and is used to write, via its **append( )** method, text to an output stream. An example of this use is featured in Section 9.4.

9.3 Sending a message to a remote computer

In principle, sending messages to remote computers is no more complicated than dealing with local I/O. The only complexity involved is in addressing the computer.

Every computer connected to the Internet has a unique IP (Internet Protocol) address. This is a sequence of four four-digit numbers describing the network the computer is part of, and the actual computer itself. This address is commonly represented as a *host name* – for example, **chroma.demon.co.uk** represents the IP address of my computer. The computer requires the numerical version of the address for communication; it can get this by a process known as *DNS lookup*.

9.3.1 DNS Lookup

Every network has access to a domain name server (DNS). This computer keeps a list of known addresses and their numerical counterparts, allowing us to quiz DNS for the numerical data our program needs to connect to a server.

We will now write a simple program to discover the IP address of a known computer. The class we will use to do this comes from **java.net** and is called **InetAddress**. This class provides a handy method called **getByName(String Hostname)**, which returns the IP address of the host name.

```
import java.net.*;

class HostName
{
    public static void main(String[] args)
    {
        try
        {
            // create an InetAddress object called host
            InetAddress host = InetAddress.getByName(" insert
                host name here eg. ChrisWright.co.uk ");

            // print out the name and IP address
            System.out.println(host);
```

```
      }
      catch(UnknownHostException e)
      {
         System.out.println("Cannot find IP number");
      }
   }
}
```

We now know how to address a remote computer, and we know that the computer has to be listening for a communication, but how does it know which communication is which? After all, a web server serves up thousands of pages daily, how will it deal with different kinds of request?

Obviously a server is not sitting waiting to process somebody else's keyboard strokes. To communicate between two computers, we need a software program dedicated to listening for a particular type of communication. We can write this ourselves, or we can make use of one of a number of well-known programs that are resident on most web servers, for example *Echo*, which is used in the real world to test that a particular server is alive. The program does exactly what the programs we wrote earlier do – echoes the keyboard strokes back to the sending computer.

To differentiate between incoming signals, computers use a method involving *ports* and *sockets*.

9.3.2 Ports and sockets

Every computer communicates through a *port*. Ports are numbered and when we send a message to an Echo client, we address it to a particular port number (Echo = Port 7). When an Echo server listening on Port 7 receives a message from a remote computer, it creates a *socket* through which all subsequent communication is made, using the remote computer's IP address and port number as a unique identifier for the session. It then goes back to listening at the port for the next computer to make contact. While this is going on, it may also be listening on port 80 for http requests for web pages. A single port can create many sockets and in certain protocols, such as ftp, a second port is used to act as a control channel. This method is used by all computers and is the reason that we can open several different web pages simultaneously or download e-mail at the same time as web pages. All these transactions will occur on different port numbers.

9.3.3 Protocols

A *protocol* in computer communications is an agreement between two ends of a communication that data will be treated in a certain way, and that the business of transferring the data will be carried out in a specified way. The Internet uses a number of protocols, the most familiar of which will be http and ftp, which are application layer protocols, or TCP and udp, which are transport layer protocols. Other examples include smtp and pop3 – the e-mail protocols – and IP, the Internet protocol.

HTTP

Hypertext transfer protocol (http) is the standard that specifies how communication occurs between a browser and a server, across the Internet. The prefix http:// that is found at the beginning of a URL is no more than an instruction to the application that this is the protocol to be used. The command

    http://www.chroma.demon.uk/tyj/examples/DragRace.html

that is sent to a server requesting a web page can be loosely translated as:

GET, using http, the page: *DragRace.html*; residing in the directory *examples*, under *tyj*, in the computer *chroma* in the *demon* network.

The URL itself breaks down into a protocol specifier, http:, the address of a web server (in this case the one at Demon Internet, where I have an account) and the directory and filename requested. In response to such a request, the server sends a message containing the response code (usually OK), the MIME type and length of file followed by the data contained in the file itself.

FTP

File transfer protocol (FTP) specifies how a file is transferred between two end points. This is used when an application is downloaded from the Net, or when you upload web pages to a server.

TCP

Transmission control protocol (TCP) is a stream-based, connection-oriented protocol that provides part of the delivery system of the Internet. Often messages from the application layer such as ftp will be encapsulated within a tcp segment, which carries the port number of the other end point. This segment will be encapsulated within an IP packet, which carries the Internet address of the remote computer.

IP

IP is a packet-oriented, connectionless protocol that deals in computer-to-computer communication. Combined with TCP, a message can be delivered to a specific port number on any computer attached to the Internet.

For an example, we are going to demonstrate the ease with which the Java stream paradigm can be used to perform TCP connections.

9.4 The Echo client

The following program uses TCP, which is a stream-oriented protocol used by nearly every Internet application. TCP works in the same way as a telephone call. A connection is made and communication happens across the connection for the duration of the call. This is why TCP is known as a *connection-oriented protocol*. Briefly, TCP works by call and response – it sends a request to open a connection to the server on the specified port. The server acknowledges and the connection is opened. When data is sent using TCP, all the error checking is done by the protocol, so we don't need to check that the message is intact. All we need to do is to implement the data processing and the initial setting up of the connection.

We know how to address an application and a computer and, given that the Echo server is run on Port 7, we can write an application to connect to an Echo server on a remote host. Because of the security restrictions on applets, if we wrote this program as an applet it would be able to contact only the server from which it is served. The following program uses **DataInputStream** to read input from the server; the **DataInputStream** is passed to an **InputStreamReader** and in turn to a **BufferedReader** to enable us to use the **readLine( )** method. A **PrintWriter** is used to write the data to the socket. The socket itself comes from the **Socket** class, which hides much of the complexity of network programming from us.

The TextField has registered with an ActionListener so that when the carriage return is pressed at the end of the line the text is copied from the field to the output Stream and the field is rendered blank.

```
import java.io.*;
import java.net.*;
import java.awt.*;
import java.awt.event.*;
import javax.swing.*;

public class WinEchoClient extends JFrame
{
    private JTextArea output;
    private JTextField input;
    private Socket theSocket;
    private String hostname;
    private String theLine;
    private BufferedReader in;
    private PrintWriter out;

    public WinEchoClient()
    {
        super("Echo Client" );
        Container c = getContentPane();
        c.add("Center", output = new JTextArea() );
        output.setEditable(false);
        input = new JTextField();
        input.addActionListener(new ActionListener(){
            public void actionPerformed(ActionEvent e)
            {
                out.println(input.getText());
                // flush the contents – force the characters out
                out.flush();
                input.setText("");
            }
        });
        c.add ("South", input );
```

```java
        this.addWindowListener(new WindowAdapter(){
          public void windowClosing(WindowEvent e)
          {
             System.exit(0);
          }
        });
    }

    public void runClient()
    {
       hostname = "localhost";

       try
       {
          theSocket = new Socket (hostname, 9999);
          output.append("Created Socket\n");

          in = new BufferedReader(new
             InputStreamReader(theSocket.getInputStream( )));
          output.append("Created DataInputStream\n");
          out = new PrintWriter(theSocket.getOutputStream( ));
          output.append("Created PrintStream\n");

          while (true)
          {
             String line = in.readLine();
             output.append("Message from Server is: " + line +
                "\n");
          }
       }
       catch (UnknownHostException e)
       {
          System.err.println(e);
       }
       catch (IOException e)
       {
          System.err.println(e);
       }
    }
    public static void main(String[] args)
    {
```

```
      WinEchoClient w = new WinEchoClient();
      w.setSize(200,200);
      w.setVisible(true);
      w.runClient();
   }
}
```

It is important to realize that not all servers run the Echo program. If you have difficulty finding one that does, we can set up a server locally, just to demonstrate this program.

9.5 The Echo server

This program is a bare-bones example, just to demonstrate the communication between processes. Firstly we need a different kind of Socket, a *serverSocket*. **serverSocket** takes a **port** number as an argument and simply listens at that port for communication. We create a serverSocket on port 9999. This is a randomly chosen number that is guaranteed to be unused – it is not allocated to any known program.

This arrangement requires that the client program is modified to connect to hostname 'localhost' on port 9999. The hostname 'localhost' returns the address 127.0.0.1 which means 'this computer'. It causes the message to be looped back to the computer it originated from and is commonly used to test communications programs.

Once the serverSocket has been set up, we listen at Port 9999 for a message. When one arrives we set up a socket to deal with it, using the line:

```
   clientSocket = echoServer.accept( );
```

allowing the serverSocket to return to listening. Having set up the socket, we need to process the data. Because the function of the program is merely to echo the data back to the sender, all we need is to set up, identically to the client program, **BufferedReader** to handle the incoming traffic and a **PrintWriter** to handle the 'echo'. Once we have done this, we simply write the incoming data straight to the socket:

```
   s = in.readLine( );
   out.println(s);
```

Note that this server will accept connections from remote machines, but it will not deal with more than one connection at a time unless we create a separate thread for the server to run new sockets in.

```java
import java.io.*;
import java.net.*;

public class EchoServer
{
    public static void main(String[] args)
    {
        // declare local variables
        ServerSocket echoServer = null;
        Socket clientSocket = null;
        BufferedReader in;
        PrintWriter out;
        String s;
// fire up the server, catching IOException in case of problems
        try
        {
            echoServer = new ServerSocket(9999);
        }
        catch (IOException e)
        {
            System.out.println(e.getMessage( ));
        }
        if (echoServer != null)
        {
            System.out.println("EchoServer listening on port 9999");
        }

        /* create a new socket for incoming transactions and
        Streams to handle data */

        try
        {
            clientSocket = echoServer.accept( );
            in = new BufferedReader(new
                InputStreamReader(clientSocket.getInputStream( )));
            out = new PrintWriter(clientSocket.getOutputStream());
            // if socket created, print out details
```

```
        while (true)
        {
            System.out.println("Message Received From:" +
                clientSocket.getInetAddress( ) + "\nFrom Port: "
            + clientSocket.getPort( ));
            // send input to output!
            s = in.readLine( );
            System.out.println(s);
            out.println(s);
            out.flush();
        }
    }
    catch (IOException e)
    {
        System.out.println(e.getMessage( ));
    }
  }
}
```

9.5.1 Multi-threaded Echo server

To make this program more lifelike, we need it to be able to handle
multiple connections, to create a number of sockets and process the
transaction for each one. To make this possible we need to have both
the **serverSocket** and the transaction processing run in their own
threads. As the class does not extend any other class, we can simply
subclass **Thread** directly. Notice how the initialization is placed in the
constructor for the class, the work is done by the **run( )** method.

We actually create two separate classes in this program. The Transaction
class does all the data processing. A new instance of Transaction is
created for each connection and run in a separate thread. The computer
runs both classes simultaneously.

```java
import java.io.*;
import java.net.*;

public class ThreadEchoServer
{
    /* declare classes - if we wanted to extend this class,
        private should be changed to protected so that the
        subclass can access these objects. */
```

```java
    private ServerSocket echoServer = null;
    private Socket clientSocket = null;
    private int i = 1;

    public ThreadEchoServer( )
    {
       try
       {
          echoServer = new ServerSocket(9999);
       }
       catch (IOException e)
       {
          System.out.println(e.getMessage( ));
       }
       System.out.println(" EchoServer listening on port 9999");

       try
       {
          while(true)
          {
             clientSocket = echoServer.accept( );
          /* hand over processing to new transaction    object
           * This part happens in as many threads as we have
           * connections */
             Transaction t = new Transaction(clientSocket);
             // print out a number for this transaction
             System.out.println("Transaction: " + i + " created");
             i++;
          }
       }
       catch (IOException e)
       {
          System.out.println(e.getMessage( ));
       }
    }

    // instantiate object
    public static void main(String[] args)
    {
       new ThreadEchoServer( );
    }
}
```

```java
// this class handles the actual data processing
class Transaction extends Thread
{
   private Socket client;
   private BufferedReader in;
   private PrintWriter out;

   // constructor to initialzse objects
   public Transaction(Socket clientSocket)
   {
      client = clientSocket;
      try
      {
         in = new BufferedReader(new
            InputStreamReader(client.getInputStream( )));
         out = new PrintWriter(client.getOutputStream( ));
      }
      catch(IOException e)
      {
         System.out.println(e.getMessage());
      }
      this.start( );
   }

   // run method handles the data
   public void run( )
   {
      String s;
      try
      {
         while (true)
         {
            System.out.println("Message Received From:" +
               client.getInetAddress()+ "\nFrom Port: " +
            client.getPort( ));

            s = in.readLine( );
            out.println(s);
            out.flush();
         }
      }
```

```
      catch(IOException e)
      {
          System.out.println(e.getMessage( ));
      }
    }
}
```

Now that we have written an application that can send and receive messages across the Internet, we can go on to something a little more interesting, retrieving data from the Internet using http.

9.6 The http client

Http is the means by which web browsers download web pages from the Internet. It is not terribly difficult in Java to write a simple client that provides the basic functionality of a web browser by downloading text/HTML files from the Internet, and reporting the status of the transaction back to the user with the response from the server. We can also use the java.net package to find out the content type of the file, its length and the date it was last modified.

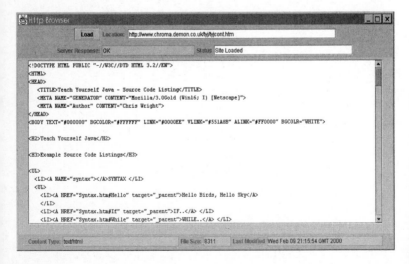

Figure 9.1 The http browser

This program is an application, because an application allows us to contact any server on the Internet. It is written using the **HttpURLConnection** class which was introduced in JDK 1.1. This class is a specialized version of **URLConnection**, and allows us to trap the response from the http server at the other end of the connection, in addition to finding out data about the file we are downloading. Because we are interested only in textual data, we will use the character-based I/O streams from **java.io**. We will also use anonymous inner classes to deal with our event handling.

The user types a URL into the location field and clicks on the 'Load' button. The Java classes save us from coding the fine details of the transaction, but they do allow us to trap some information about the file. This can be displayed in **textField**s.

```java
import java.io.*;
import java.net.*;
import java.awt.*;
import java.awt.event.*;
import javax.swing.*;
import java.util.*;

class Browser extends JFrame
{
    // declare all HCI elements
    private JLabel locLabel, responseLabel,statusLabel,
    typeLabel, sizeLabel, modifiedLabel;
    private JTextField locDisplay, response, status,
    contentType, size, modified;
    private JButton b;
    private JScrollPane displayHolder;
    private JTextArea display;
    private ActionListener l;

    public Browser( )
    {
        Container c = getContentPane();
        this.setTitle("Http Browser");

        JPanel p = new JPanel( );
        p.setLayout(new BorderLayout());
```

```java
    JPanel pa = new JPanel( );
    pa.setBackground(Color.lightGray);
    responseLabel = new JLabel("Server Response:");
    response = new JTextField(20);
    response.setEditable(false);
    statusLabel = new JLabel("Status");
    status = new JTextField(30);
    pa.add(responseLabel);
    pa.add(response);
    pa.add(statusLabel);
    pa.add(status);

    JPanel pb = new JPanel( );
    /* To handle pages of unknown length, we need to
 *  create a scrollable area – use a text area to define the
 *  size of the viewable area and pass it to a ScrollPane
 *  object – this has its own layout manager which handles
 *  the scroll */

    display = new JTextArea(20,120);
    displayHolder = new JScrollPane(display);
    Font f = new Font("Courier", Font.PLAIN, 12);
    display.setFont(f);
    display.setEditable(false);
    pb.add(displayHolder);

    p.add("North", pa);
    p.add("Center", pb);

    JPanel p1 = new JPanel( );
    b = new JButton("Load");
    l = new Loader( );
    b.addActionListener(l);

    locLabel = new JLabel("Location: ");
    locDisplay = new JTextField(45);

    p1.setBackground(Color.lightGray);
    p1.add(b);
    p1.add(locLabel);
    p1.add(locDisplay);
```

```
      JPanel p2 = new JPanel( );
      typeLabel = new JLabel("Content Type:");
      contentType = new JTextField(25);
      contentType.setEditable(false);
      sizeLabel = new JLabel("File Size:");
      size = new JTextField(6);
      size.setEditable(false);
      modifiedLabel = new JLabel("Last Modified");
      modified = new JTextField(25);
      modified.setEditable(false);
      p2.setBackground(Color.lightGray);
      p2.add(typeLabel);
      p2.add(contentType);
      p2.add(sizeLabel);
      p2.add(size);
      p2.add(modifiedLabel);
      p2.add(modified);

      c.add("Center", p);
      c.add("North", p1);
      c.add("South", p2);

      this.addWindowListener(new WindowAdapter( ){
         public void windowClosing(WindowEvent e)
         {
            System.exit(0);
         }
      }); //end inner class declaration
   }

   public static void main(String[] args)
   {
      JFrame f = new Browser( );
      f.setSize(900,500);
      f.setVisible(true);
   }

   // inner class definition – substantial amount of code here
   class Loader implements ActionListener
   {
      public void actionPerformed(ActionEvent e)
```

```java
{
   URL target = null;
   String contents = null;
   String type = null;
   String server = null;
   Date date = null;
   int length = 0;

    // start the loop
   try
   {
      // read in the user's text from the location field
      target = new URL(locDisplay.getText( ));

      // let user know that we are doing something!
      status.setText("Finding: "+ target);

      /* initialize an HttpURLConnection object when
      * connection is available */

      HttpURLConnection fetch =
         (HttpURLConnection)target.openConnection( );

      // use HttpURLConnection object to get response
      server = fetch.getResponseMessage( );

      // pass the response to the display for the user
      response.setText(server);

      BufferedReader in = new BufferedReader(new
         InputStreamReader(fetch.getInputStream( )));

      // Let user know that we are receiving data
      status.setText("Loading Pages now...");
      display.setText("");

      /* prepare a character array to hold 1Kb of data
   * from Buffered Reader */

      char[] buffer = new char[1024];
      int charsRead;
```

```java
// read it in from the BufferedReader to the character array
        while((charsRead = in.read(buffer, 0, 1024)) != -1)
        {
            // put character data into a String
        contents = new String(buffer, 0, charsRead);
            display.append(contents);
        }

        /* leaving this loop requires in.read( ) to return -1,
         * which implies there is no more data being
    * transferred so we assume that all the text has
         * been transferred */

        status.setText("Site Loaded");

        // interrogate inputstream headers
        type = fetch.getContentType( );
        length = fetch.getContentLength( );
        date = new Date(fetch.getLastModified( ));

        // print information to appropriate textField
        contentType.setText(type);
        size.setText(Integer.toString(length));
        modified.setText(date.toString());
    }
    // just in case.....
    catch(MalformedURLException ex)
    {
        System.out.println(ex.getMessage( ));
    }
    catch(IOException ex)
    {
        System.out.println(ex.getMessage( ));
    }
    } // end method
  } // end inner class
} // end class
```

SUMMARY

✓ This chapter demonstrates the ease with which Java can be used to do a variety of networking jobs. It provides a basic introduction to the principles of data communication and client server programming.

✓ The Java.net.Socket class provides a quick and easy solution that will implement network connections regardless of platform. We don't have to worry if the remote computer is using Unix, Windows or Macintosh as a platform; the JVM for that particular platform will ensure compliance.

✓ The Echo client and server establishes very basic principles. It doesn't take a huge stretch of the imagination to work out how the two programmes freatured here could be altered to provide the basics of a 'chat' programme or Bulletin Board.

✓ The http browser similarly could be converted into a text-only web browser by stripping the HTML characters out of the text.

Exercises

❶ Rewrite the server programs giving them GUIs displaying messages in **TextAreas**.

❷ Rewrite the clients so that the transaction is triggered by pressing a button rather than the carriage return.

❸ Write code that allows the client to close the connection by sending an agreed word or character (such as Quit or Bye). The server should send the client the instructions for closing the socket at connection time, so that the user will know how to close it down gracefully (the code to close the socket is **mySocket.close( );**).

❹ Find out what other information can be discovered about a URL and implement a means of retrieving and displaying it (hint: **HttpURLConnection** is derived from **URLConnection**).

10 DRAG RACING – THE GAME

AIMS OF THIS CHAPTER

The aim of this chapter is to deliver a working model of the drag racing game. The code for the GUI we have already developed, and is the same code as we have seen elsewhere in the book. However, we still need to provide automotive powers to the cars and synchronize the race with the betting.

The code as presented here is not a finished version of the game. At the end of the chapter I will suggest some structural improvements that you should be able to implement. When you have done that you will have developed a full-scale working applet that can be embedded in web pages and released to the Internet.

Note that the class and image files are deployed as a 'jar' or Java archive file. This is a compressed file designed to reduce access time over the Internet. To create a jar file simply open a DOS window, navigate to a directory containing only the Class and image files you wish to distribute and type:

    jar cf RaceTrack.jar *.*

where RaceTrack.jar is the name of the archive you intend to distribute.

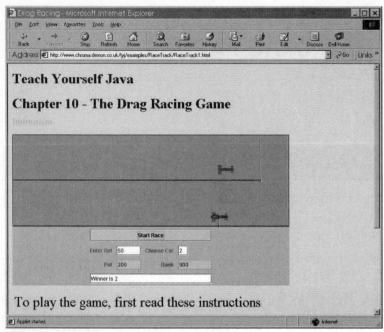

Figure 10.1 Drag racing in the browser

10.1 The web page

We must supply some instructions to the players, and a good place to do this is the Web page in which the finished applet will be embedded.

The applet is embedded in the web page with this HTML code. Note that we use both the OBJECT and the EMBED tags so that the applet will play in both Internet Explorer and Netscape – the *classid* attribute refers to the Java2 plug-in which enables the browser to display an applet written with Swing components. If the browser is unable to find the plug-in it will download it from the supplied URL.

```
<OBJECT classid= "clsid:8AD9C840-044E-11D1-B3E9-
00805F499D93" WIDTH = "650" HEIGHT = "350" codebase=
"http://java.sun.com/products/plugin/1.2/jinstall-12-
win32.cab#Version=1,2,0,0">
<PARAM NAME = CODE VALUE = "RaceTrack.class" >
```

```
<PARAM NAME = CODEBASE VALUE = "." >
<PARAM NAME = ARCHIVE VALUE = "RaceTrack.jar" >
<PARAM NAME= "type" VALUE="application/x-java-
applet;version=1.2">
<COMMENT>
<EMBED type= "application/x-java-applet;version=1.2"
java_CODE = "RaceTrack.class" java_CODEBASE = "."
java_ARCHIVE = "RaceTrack.jar" WIDTH = "650" HEIGHT = "350"
pluginspage= "http://java.sun.com/products/plugin/1.2/
plugin-install.html">
<NOEMBED></COMMENT></NOEMBED>
</EMBED>
</OBJECT>
```

10.2 The program logic

The program consists of two classes, one of which 'contains' the other (the applet **RaceTrack** is a container for the **RaceTrackPanel** class).

RaceTrack sets up the screen elements, downloads the image files and triggers the initialization of the **RaceTrackPanel.** In addition to this, it runs the betting part of the game in a similar manner to our dummy run earlier in the book.

RaceTrackPanel implements the **Runnable** interface in order to drive the animation. This causes the screen to be redrawn by successive calls to **paintComponent( )** generated by the thread. The thread is started by the user clicking the "Start Race" button. An incrementing counter in Thread is used to supply the x position of the cars along the track, in combination with a random number between 0 and 5 which causes them to move at different speeds and allows one to catch up and over-take the other.

The **RaceTrackPanel** class is passed a reference to the applet so that we can send the current position of the cars back to see if we have a winner. The position of each car is sent back to the **isWinner(int x, int y)** method of the **RaceTrack** class every time **paintComponent( )** is called. When both cars have passed the finishing line, the thread is stopped and the winnings and losses are administered.

10.3 The code

This is the complete code.

```java
import java.awt.*;
import java.awt.event.*;
import javax.swing.*;

public class RaceTrack extends JApplet
{
   private RaceTrackPanel animation;
   private JLabel betLabel, potLabel, bankLabel, carLabel;
   private JTextField betField, carField, potField, bankField,
winnerField;
   private JButton goButton;
   private JPanel p;

   public void init( )
   {
      Image Track =
         getImage(getDocumentBase(),"Track.gif");
      Image Car1 =
         getImage(getDocumentBase(),"RedCar.gif");
      Image Car2 =
         getImage(getDocumentBase(),"BlueCar.gif");
      animation = new RaceTrackPanel(this, Track, Car1, Car2);
      Container c = getContentPane();

      c.setLayout(new BorderLayout( ));
      p = new JPanel( );
      p.setBackground(Color.lightGray);
      GridBagLayout grid = new GridBagLayout();
      p.setLayout(grid);
      betLabel = new JLabel("Enter Bet");
      carLabel = new JLabel( "Choose Car");
      potLabel = new JLabel("Pot");
      bankLabel = new JLabel("Bank");

      betField = new JTextField(5);
      carField = new JTextField(2);
      potField = new JTextField(5);
```

```
bankField = new JTextField(7);
winnerField = new JTextField(20);

potField.setEditable( false );
bankField.setEditable( false );

goButton = new JButton("Start Race");
goButton.addActionListener(new ActionListener(){
   public void actionPerformed(ActionEvent e)
   {
      animation.start( );
   }
});

GridBagConstraints gbc = new GridBagConstraints( );

gbc.fill = GridBagConstraints.BOTH;
gbc.insets = new Insets(5, 5, 5, 5);
gblAdd(goButton, grid, gbc, 0, 0, 4, 1);

gbc.fill = GridBagConstraints.NONE;
gbc.anchor = GridBagConstraints.EAST;
gblAdd(betLabel, grid, gbc, 0, 1, 1, 1);

gbc.anchor = GridBagConstraints.WEST;
gblAdd(betField, grid, gbc, 1, 1, 1, 1);

gbc.anchor = GridBagConstraints.EAST;
gblAdd(carLabel, grid, gbc, 2, 1, 1, 1);

gbc.anchor = GridBagConstraints.WEST;
gblAdd(carField, grid, gbc, 3, 1, 1, 1);

gbc.anchor = GridBagConstraints.EAST;
gblAdd(potLabel, grid, gbc, 0, 2, 1, 1);

gbc.anchor = GridBagConstraints.WEST;
gblAdd(potField, grid, gbc, 1, 2, 1, 1);

gbc.anchor = GridBagConstraints.EAST;
gblAdd(bankLabel, grid, gbc,2, 2, 1, 1);

gbc.anchor = GridBagConstraints.WEST;
gblAdd(bankField, grid, gbc, 3, 2, 1, 1);
```

```java
            gbc.fill = GridBagConstraints.BOTH;
            gblAdd(winnerField, grid, gbc, 0, 3, 4, 1);

            betField.setText("");
            potField.setText("100");
            bankField.setText("1000");

            c.add("Center", animation);
            c.add("South", p);
        }

        private void gblAdd(Component c, GridBagLayout
        grid,GridBagConstraints gbc, int x, int y, int w, int h)
        {
            gbc.gridx = x;
            gbc.gridy = y;
            gbc.gridwidth = w;
            gbc.gridheight = h;
            grid.setConstraints( c, gbc);
            p.add(c);
        }

    // Check to see which car wins (Called from RaceTrackPanel)
      public void Winner(int x, int y)
      {
         if ((x > y) && (y > 550))
         {
            play(1);
            animation.stop();
         }
         else if ((y>x) && (x > 560))
         {
            play(2);
            animation.stop();
         }
         else if ((x==y) && (x >560))
         {
            winnerField.setText("Dead Heat!");
            animation.stop();
         }
      }
```

```java
      // Administer winnings and losses
      public void play(int x)
      {
         int bet, pot, bank, car, result;

         winnerField.setText("");
         bet = Integer.parseInt(betField.getText( ));
         pot = Integer.parseInt(potField.getText( ));
         bank = Integer.parseInt(bankField.getText( ));
         car = Integer.parseInt(carField.getText( ));

         result = x;
         winnerField.setText("Winner is " + Integer.toString( result));

         if (result == car)
         {
            pot = pot + bet;
            potField.setText( Integer.toString( pot));
            bank = bank - bet;
            bankField.setText( Integer.toString( bank));
         }
         else
         {
            pot = pot - bet;
            potField.setText( Integer.toString( pot));
            bank = bank + bet;
            bankField.setText( Integer.toString( bank));
         }
      }
   }

   // A Panel is required to display the graphics
   class RaceTrackPanel extends JPanel implements Runnable
   {
      RaceTrack app;
      public Thread driver = null;
      Image Track, Car1, Car2;
      int XPos1,XPos2, YPos, progress, speed1, speed2;

      public RaceTrackPanel(RaceTrack parent, Image Track,
         Image Car1, Image Car2)
```

```java
{
   setSize(600,270);
   setBackground(Color.darkGray);
   app = parent;

   this.Track = Track;
   this.Car1 = Car1;
   this.Car2 = Car2;

   // initial position of cars
   XPos1 = 30;
   XPos2 = 30;
   YPos = 55;

   // start race at beginning
   progress = -1;
}

// Reposition cars and (re)start thread
public void start( )
{
   if (driver == null)
   {
      XPos1 = 30;
      XPos2 = 30;
      driver = new Thread(this);
      driver.start( );
   }
}

public void stop( )
{
   driver = null;
}

public void run( )
{
   while( driver != null)
   {
      // compute random number to move cars
      speed1 = (int)Math.floor(Math.random( )*5);
```

```
      speed2 = (int)Math.floor(Math.random( )*5);

      // increment counter and call paintComponent( )
      progress++;
      try
      {
        repaint( );
        Thread.sleep(250);
      }
      catch(InterruptedException e)
      {
        System.out.println(e.getMessage( ));
      }
    }
  }

  // Pass the speed variables into the drawing method
  public void paintComponent(Graphics g)
  {
    super.paintComponent(g);
    paintRace(g, speed1, speed2);
  }

  public void paintRace(Graphics g, int x, int y)
  {
    int w, h;
    w = Track.getWidth(app);
    h = Track.getHeight(app);
    if ((w>0) && (h>0))
    {
      System.out.println("loading Track");
      g.drawImage(Track, 0, 0, this);
      System.out.println("Track loaded");
    }
    w = Car1.getWidth(app);
    h = Car2.getHeight(app);
    if ((w>0) && (h>0))
    {
      // position is current position + counter + random number
      XPos1 = XPos1 + progress + x;
```

```
        XPos2 = XPos2 + progress + y;
        g.drawImage(Car1, XPos1, YPos, this);
        System.out.println("Car1 loaded");
        g.drawImage(Car2, XPos2, YPos +105, this);
        System.out.println("Car2 loaded");
        // Send current position to Winner method for checking
        app.Winner(XPos1, XPos2);
    }
  } // end of method
} // end of class
```

10.4 Developing the program

The featured code is passable as a prototype, but there are many improvements that could be made to make the program more realistic, as well as more robust.

For realism, if we were to make a separate class for the car, with its own drawing methods, we could easily make the application more lifelike by introducing skids (swapping for a rotated image) and give the car a range of user-selectable attributes geared to the performance. We could elegantly introduce different patterns of acceleration by triggering an additional random number to be added after a certain **Xpos** has passed. We could also introduce a sound file to play for the duration of the game. Try adjusting the scope of the random number, which may give more dramatic overtaking manoeuvres, but if increased too far will detract from the program's smoothness.

It would be relatively simple to make the track rectangular and have the cars do laps. The trick here is to substitute a rotated version of the car image and to shift the increment from Xpos to Ypos when a certain position is reached.

To speed the race up, implement it using clipping so that we don't redraw the background each time, and make the delay on the thread smaller.

For robustness, the essential thing is to make sure that the user inputs some numerical data, or to provide code that will do it but not count it as a valid bet. The reason for this is that we are passing the values in the fields, via a conversion routine, back into the program. If there is no value in the field, we will get runtime errors.

At this point, we have moved suddenly into the realm of real-world applications – you are now ready to take on the whole language. Remember that the Java API, often bundled with the distribution, will yield answers to most of your queries, as long as you understand what you are trying to do. If the logic is wrong, nothing will save the program except patience, calm and a willingness to go back and start again.

APPENDICES

1 Java keywords

Keywords are reserved for specific purposes in a programming language and are not allowed for use as variable names.

abstract	final	protected
boolean	finally	public
break	float	return
byte	for	short
byvalue	goto	static
case	if	super
catch	implements	switch
char	import	synchronised
class	instanceof	this
const	int	threadsafe
continue	interface	throw
default	long	transient
do	native	true
double	new	try
else	null	void
extends	package	while
false	private	

2 Internet resources

Web sites

The web is an ever-changing medium, and there are literally hundreds of web sites with Java applets featured. I have restricted this list to a level higher, and these sites can be looked on as gateways. If you know of any excellent site that has been omitted from this list, please email me at:

tyj@chroma.demon.co.uk

http://www.chroma.demon.co.uk/
Contains a link to the site supporting this book and many more Java-related sites.

http://www.javaworld.com/javasoft.index.html
A superb resource. Magazine format contains code, advice, discussion.

http://java.sun.com/docs/books/tutorial/
Java tutorial with Sun's blessing.

http://www.geocities.com/Athens/7077/scoop/onjava.html
Dick Baldwin's Java Programming Tutorials.

http://www.neca.com/~vmis/java.html
Shlurrrp....Java tutorial.

http://www.progsource.com/java.html
The programmer's source....

http://www.developer.com/
The front door to the legendary Gamelan site.

http://javaboutique.internet.com/
The Java boutique.

http://www.apl.jhu.edu/~hall/java/Welcome.html
Java programming resources.

http://www.seajug.org/html/resources.html
Java related resources.

http://n106.is.tokushima-u.ac.jp/member/kita/info/java.html
Java resources (Japan).

http://www.acme.com/java/
ACME Java – excellent and informative resource.

http://www.infospheres.caltech.edu/resources/java.html
Java resources at Caltech – extensive and very useful.

News groups

Of the many Java newsgroups, the two listed below stand out for being tolerant towards newcomers and having a large enough flow of traffic to remain interesting.

comp.lang.java.gui

comp.lang.java.programmer

Advice to beginners

Just hang out and read the messages for a few days at first – the chances are that something similar will have already been asked. One good way to earn the hatred of everyone on a list is to ask one of the FAQ questions. To avoid this, seek out and read the FAQs for each list you subscribe to.

INDEX